BERKLEE PRESS

MANAGE Your STRESS and PAIN through MUSIC

Dr. Suzanne B. Hanser
Dr. Susan E. Mandel

Illustrated by Louisa Bertman
Edited by Jonathan Feist

This book is not intended to replace expert medical advice. The authors
and the publisher urge you to verify the appropriateness of any procedure
or exercise with your qualified health care professional. The authors and the
publisher disclaim any liability or loss, personal or otherwise, resulting from
the procedures and information in this book.

Berklee Press

Vice President: David Kusek
Dean of Continuing Education: Debbie Cavalier
Chief Operating Officer: Robert F. Green
Managing Editor: Jonathan Feist
Editorial Assistants: Emily Goldstein, Yousun Choi, Martin Fowler, Amy Kaminski, Jacqueline Sim

ISBN 978-0-87639-101-3

DISTRIBUTED BY

HAL•LEONARD®

1140 Boylston Steet
Boston, MA 02215-3693 USA
(617) 747-2146
Visit Berklee Press Online at:
www.berkleepress.com

7777 W. BLUEMOUND RD. P.O. BOX 13819
MILWAUKEE, WISCONSIN 53213
Visit Hal Leonard Online at:
www.halleonard.com

In memory of Samuel Benjamin Hanser
Healer of Stress and Pain
1982–2010

CONTENTS

CD TRACKS

1   "Take a Deep Breath." Susan E. Mandel, guide.

2   "Bonsai." Original improvisation by Suzanne B. Hanser. Assisted by Raviva Hanser, Tova Teperow, Shelley Tsao, and Amanda Maestro-Scherer, hand chimes.

3   "A Musical Workout" (introduction). Suzanne B. Hanser, guide.

4   "Traumerai" by Robert Schumann. Suzanne B. Hanser, piano.

5   "A Musical Workout" (conclusion). Suzanne B. Hanser, guide.

6   "A Musical Massage." Suzanne B. Hanser, guide.

7   "Sequoia." Original improvisation by Suzanne B. Hanser, Native American flute.

8   "Building a Bond with Music." Suzanne B. Hanser, guide.

9   "To a Wild Rose" by Edward MacDowell. Suzanne B. Hanser, piano.

10   "La Fille aux Cheveau de Lin" by Claude Debussy. Suzanne B. Hanser, piano.

11   "Finding Inner Harmony"
     • "Gymnopedie #1" from *Trois Gymnopedies* by Erik Satie. Daniel Kobialka, music; Susan E. Mandel, guide.[1]

12   "Sensing Peaceful Images" (introduction). Suzanne B. Hanser, guide.

13   "Clair de Lune" by Claude Debussy. Suzanne B. Hanser, therapeutic harp.

14   "Sensing Peaceful Images" (conclusion). Suzanne B. Hanser, guide.

15   "Discovering Your Imagination"
     • "Lullaby" by Daniel Kobialka. Daniel Kobialka, music; Susan E. Mandel, guide.[2]

16   "Lullaby" (music only) from *Timeless Motion* by Daniel Kobialka.[3]

Guided facilitation mixed by Chee-Ping Ho.

Hanser performances produced by Rob Jaczko.

---

[1] "Trois Gymnopedies" from *Fragrances of a Dream*, © Daniel Kobialka (BMI), www.wonderofsound.com.

[2] Lullaby from *Timeless Motion*, © Daniel Kobialka (BMI), www.wonderfsound.com.

[3] © Daniel Kobialka (BMI), www.wonderfsound.com.

FOREWORD

Are you feeling stressed, overwhelmed, out of control? Are you constantly multitasking? Is this stress taking a toll on your physical and psychological well-being? Do you suffer from insomnia, headaches, hypertension, IBS, chronic pain, anxiety, irritability, or feeling "down in the dumps?" If you answered "Yes" to any of these symptoms (or you may have others), you and this book will become best friends.

This book offers the perfect antidote for many of the struggles and challenges of life: *music*. It encourages you to listen and interact with music and notice how it affects you, to go beyond your limitations in reducing stress and controlling pain, and to find your own inner harmony.

In a deeply personal way, the two gifted authors tell the stories of how they experienced the healing powers of music for their own health challenges. These experiences inspired each of them to pursue music therapy as a career.

They have years of clinical experience with a variety of patients and stories that they share with us. I have had the privilege of working with both authors to observe their skills. They have also conducted brilliant research to verify the power and efficacy of music therapy in the health-care setting. Now, in a conversational form—as if they were right in the room with the reader—they are giving their wisdom to all of us.

You will have so much fun with this book. It comes with a CD, and the authors offer a variety of music programs to use in everyday life or for specific situations and conditions. You can explore singing, chanting, instrument playing, moving to the music, songwriting—even silence. Just imagine! You can keep a personal "music listening log" and create your own music collection, remembering music that was meaningful to you at different times of your life and identifying music you enjoy now. You will discover how music affects your body, mood, thoughts, energy, self-esteem, concentration, and even your outlook on your future.

I personally love the chapter on the "musical workout," which combines breathing and movement to some of your favorite music. You "act out" the music to reduce tension or agitation, reduce pain, or improve your mood. Within minutes of moving to the rhythms, snapping your fingers, or dancing, you will definitely be smiling.

One Sunday, I was feeling sad and not looking forward to work on Monday. I decided to give this "musical workout" a try, to see if it would change my mood. I went to my CD collection and played the Beatles' "All You Need Is Love" at full blast, followed by Abba, then "Hey Good Lookin'" by Hank Williams, then some Irish fiddle music. In a short period of time, I felt euphoric, and the stuff that had been bothering me seemed like a piece of cake. The experience reminded me of my fear of public speaking when I first came to the Mind/Body Medicine Institute at Harvard. I found that if I listened to African drumming music or Dvorak's ninth symphony before my talks, I felt confident not only to meet the task but also to have fun.

I mentioned the authors' CD. So many people are suffering from insomnia—having trouble falling asleep or staying asleep. Listening to the "Lullaby" (track 16) could be more effective than any sleep medication, and it has no side effects.

The other thing I love about this book, that sets it apart from others, is you can start reading it wherever you want. Search through the chapters and see what speaks to you the most. Take a look at "Musical Massage" with its suggestions to listen to calming music while breathing comfortably and massaging the muscles of your scalp, forehead, around your eyes, cheeks, jaw, chin, neck, and shoulders. What a great way to begin or end your day! I personally suggest you complete the Stress Assessment Log before you read any of the chapters, so that you understand your stress warning signs—what pushes your buttons—and then evaluate the changes in your stress levels before and after your music selections.

May this inspiring book and your music experiences transport you, comfort you, turn you on—and most of all, provide healing in mind, body, and spirit.

Ann Webster, Ph.D.
Benson-Henry Institute for Mind Body Medicine
Massachusetts General Hospital
Harvard Medical School

INTRODUCTION

As future unfolds
New beginning awakens
I am there and here

—Susan E. Mandel

Music has the power to affect us deeply. It evokes our smiles and tears. It stirs memories, excites us, and soothes us. When words fail, music helps express our feelings. It guides us to relate and create. By focusing on the music within us, we can learn to look past our limitations, cope with stress, and relieve our pain.

OUR BOOK

Manage Your Stress and Pain Through Music deals with the difficulties that we all face in living a full life. We, your authors, encourage you to make music more a part of your day. Music can do many things for you: it can calm you when you are anxious, distract you from pain, or take you far away from your troubles. Music is capable of transfixing and transfusing you with energy and life. Our book shows you how to use music to cope with some of the challenges in your life. By learning to listen and to interact with music in a new way, we show you how to attend to the changes that happen to you and your stress and pain. By creating a personal music plan, you will be able to take the strategies that work for you and make them a part of your day. We hope that, in the process, you will learn how music can help you to feel more complete and fulfilled.

In part I, we build a foundation for understanding your own stress and pain, and we describe what music can do for you. In chapter 1, we introduce the research that supports the effectiveness of particular music strategies in dealing with various types of stress and pain. In chapter 2, we continue with an explanation of stress that shows how you can take control of the stressors in your life. Chapter 3 describes the inner workings of pain in order to demonstrate how your perception of pain can be modified. You will experience the opportunity to assess your personal needs and to evaluate your experiences in chapter 4. Part I is the most technical part of the book, so you may choose to scan these chapters at first, and then return to read them in more detail as you implement your personal music plan.

Part II introduces you to a compendium of music strategies that work with your body, mind, and spirit to help you manage your unique responses to stress and pain. A variety of strategies are detailed in eleven music programs, each of which is designed with a particular effect in mind. You will learn how to use music for relaxation, for attention, and for engaging your hidden creative and musical abilities. In addition, you will explore singing, chanting, instrument playing, improvisation, and songwriting, as well as the role of silence in your well-being. You will discover how to apply these music strategies to everyday life, as well as to specific situations, such as coping with medical procedures and work-related stress.

Part III asks you to review your needs and musical experiences to evaluate your personal music plan. We hope you will see such improvement that you will commit to making music an even more important part of your life.

OUR RECORDING

We hope that you will enjoy creating your own playlists or mixes to accompany the music programs. We are also delighted to bring you our original CD that includes eight selections of music. These are accompanied by verbal suggestions to reinforce the music programs you will learn in our book.

MUSIC THERAPY

Music therapy involves the planned application of music and the relationship with the therapist to promote well-being of a person's body, mind, and spirit. Following completion of a four-year accredited course of study, including music and psychology, 1200 hours of supervised clinical practice, and successful completion of an eligibility examination, music therapists become board certified by the Certification Board for Music Therapists. Music therapy is practiced in a variety of educational and healthcare settings.

YOUR AUTHORS

We bring sixty years of collective experience as professional music therapists to this book. As part of our music therapy practices, we have been fortunate to be able to use our own music talents to assist hundreds of others in managing stress and pain. In these pages, we share our knowledge of the theories behind the use of music, provide examples from our clinical and personal experience, and describe research-based music techniques that we think will make a difference in your life. But first, we would like to introduce ourselves.

A Musical Life: Suzanne B. Hanser

"Symphony"

Gathering rain clouds
My stricken body
Hears the falling notes

—Suzanne B. Hanser

I was never childish. I don't remember being childlike, but I was always frail. Illness was my companion during those years known as childhood, while I endured too many exploratory surgeries and diagnostic tests to count. It turned out that I had two congenital deformities. My bladder was shaped like a squished ball, and it stopped functioning when I was nine. I had no middle ear at all, nor a canal to transmute sound from outside in. While surgery successfully reconstructed my bladder, I still have no hearing in my left ear, despite a surgically built canal. So you see that being a child was not much fun for me.

When I was bedridden (and that was much of my young life), my mother would play her favorite recordings for me. They ran the gamut from Tchaikovsky's *Nutcracker Suite* to Ella Fitzgerald's tunes, and Frank Sinatra's croons to J.S. Bach's fugues. I could lose myself in the land of the Arabian Nights orchestrated by Rimsky-Korsakoff in his *Scheherazade*, or in the pastoral scenes of Beethoven's sixth symphony. While I listened, I was in magical places far more interesting than my bedroom. I even "forgot" the pain I was in, and the loneliness I felt because I couldn't go to school.

After my ear surgery, my parents offered to buy me a present. My choice was clear: I wanted a piano. Although it took them years to pay it off, my parents invested in my future with that purchase, and here I am, today, writing this book! That piano was my best friend, and it rang out either good cheer or deep despair, depending upon my mood. My made-up songs sang out just what I needed to say.

Perhaps it was inevitable that I would become a music therapist. I had certainly experienced the healing powers of music in my own recovery. Whether I listened, played, or sang, I felt nurtured and soothed while the music surrounded me. My record player could bring a whole orchestra to my bedside and I was grateful to hear such beautiful music anytime I wanted. When I was up to it, I could play my piano, and express things I didn't know I felt.

Later, as an adult, I learned an even more powerful lesson about the impact of music on pain. After nine healthy months of pregnancy, my water broke, and I arrived at the hospital. Nurse after nurse tried to hear a fetal heartbeat, but none could. For the next fourteen hours, I endured labor, knowing, but not really believing, that my baby would be stillborn. Fortunately, I brought my music with me. I chronicled my experience in "Childbirth, Childdeath." [1]

I selected a cassette of Mozart piano sonatas that I had played as a child. I breathed with every measure and put every bit of my concentration into following the rhythm. I focused on the notes, what they looked like on the staff, how I'd played them as a child, how my parents watched me play, and how I loved playing. My arms connected with the keys as a straw with a glass of milk, sucking in the sweet tonalities. I listened now, in the hospital, and I was there, at seven, at the keyboard, wondering how each finger followed the other so automatically, so quickly.

I breathed to Vivaldi's concerti, which had a regular beat and few harmonic surprises. It provided a respite from the physical discomfort of reality. The steadiness of the music led me back to a comforting moment. I knew that each phrase would resolve into consonance. But soon, the calm, predictable meters and progressions could not hold me down. I was breathing harder and faster as the contractions intensified. I was losing control of my breath. I was losing the ability to keep going, to keep breathing, to keep believing that a baby would be born.

[1] S. B. Hanser, "Childbirth, Childdeath," In *Educators, Therapists, and Artists on Reflective Practice*, ed. J.J.G. Byers and M. Forinash, 137–138 (New York: Peter Lang, 2004).

I had to keep myself from thinking ahead. I had to remain in the music, a world I knew and loved, and needed to inhabit at this time. The pauses between cassettes let in despair. Longer, stronger contractions signaled the transition phase of labor, the last before birth. I became terrified of what lay ahead.

Chaos and turmoil swirled and snapped around me. If music could help at all, it needed to churn with torment and drama. I had brought a recording of Prokofieff's second piano concerto. This contemporary work was full of energetic runs, loud climaxes and harmonic dissonance. I tried to identify something in the music to pull me in. Within seconds, it offered the force I needed to drive its rhythms into my psyche, to match my emotional state with its discord.... I measured the time by counting cassettes and replays. I played the Prokofieff again, and again, and again until the agony subsided. Until the contractions ended. After twenty-one recordings, it was over.

I say that music got me through that labor. I thought that if music could support me through this traumatic time, it could also assist others in coping with pain and stress in their lives. My work as a clinical music therapist and researcher has attested to this. I know that it can help you, too.

My Journey with Music: Susan E. Mandel

"immersion"

i go there to let go
mantra in my mind
shifting shades and colors
emerge behind my eyes
breathe in—exhale
steady as it deepens
body feels heavy
mind through silence listens
enter light and clarity
senses keen then blurred
kaleidoscope of fleeting
images observe
release constraint and tension
suspend my conscious mind
experience open knowing
of pleasure beyond time
i go there to let go
to allow my healing
embrace trust—release control
immersion in the being

—Susan E. Mandel

Arthritis entered my life about thirty years ago. I returned to school to complete course work to become a board-certified music therapist. Juggling my responsibilities as student, wife, and mother, I tried to disregard the neck pain and numbness that interrupted my activities. But the pain refused to be ignored, and I found myself in a spine surgeon's office, hearing the words "cervical fusion" as though the physician was talking about someone else. As my husband helped me to absorb the reality of the situation, my mind focused on overcoming this obstacle to be cured of the problem. I underwent the surgery and lengthy recuperation. Although the scar on my neck was a visible reminder of my ordeal, I returned to my busy life as though it had never happened. Two years later, I was back in the operating room for my second spinal fusion. I began to understand the implications of a degenerative condition. And so I embarked on my journey with music.

As a registered music therapist, in July 1985, I had the opportunity to successfully utilize several music therapy techniques for pain distraction, symptom control, relaxation, and expression of emotion, while a patient myself.… This was my third spine surgery, and during the prior two hospitalizations, I had not utilized any music therapy methods, giving me a basis for comparison of my subjective experience with and without the use of music.[2]

I selected tape recordings of my favorite music and brought the music, a portable cassette player, and headphones to the hospital. My husband placed the headphones on my ears while I was in the recovery room. I recall my sense of comfort that accompanied the music. I listened to the taped music each time a nurse administered pain medication.

I clearly remember the first night following both prior surgeries as having been very long and difficult. Following this surgery, with the use of music, I have no memory of any post-surgical pain during the hours required to regain full consciousness from the anesthetic. Once fully conscious, I required minimal medication for pain management.[3]

Since that time, I underwent seven additional spine surgeries, as well as multiple knee and shoulder surgeries, and countless medical tests and exams. Each experience allowed me an opportunity to experiment with music for my own wellness. I selected music to relieve my anxiety awaiting surgery, to ease the discomfort of pre-surgical procedures, to calm me in the operating room, and to arouse me comfortably from anesthesia. I recall orienting myself to time and place before I was able to communicate, as I regained consciousness in the recovery room. I recognized the mildly stimulating music that I selected to hear after the surgery was complete, and calculated the timing of the music to determine that I had been out of surgery for about thirty minutes.

Over the years, my cassette player was replaced with a portable compact disc player, and now an MP3 player accompanies me to all my medical appointments. During times of little control, I select my preferred music. I choose music to distract me—often show tunes with meaningful lyrics and associated memories. I am comforted by

[2] S. E. Mandel, "Music Therapy: A Personal Peri-surgical Experience," *Music Therapy Perspectives 5* (1998): 109.

[3] Mandel, 109.

music's presence in "Music of the Night" from *Phantom of the Opera*, and enjoy the release of "Defying Gravity" from *Wicked*. In hours of solitude, music is with me. I immerse myself in the piano music of Jim Brickman's *By Heart*, as well as James Galway's flute renditions in *The Wind Beneath My Wings*. My feelings resound with Ann Mortifee's vocal interpretation of "Born to Live." In private moments, music allows me to express pent-up emotions. Music elicits silent tears that bring relief, as I experienced following a spine surgery:

> *Alone in my room, feeling very calm and pleased to be going home two days earlier than expected, I listened to Pachelbel's* Canon in D. *Slowly, I found my pillow increasingly wet, and realized that I was crying. The crying became silent sobbing, yet I felt no sorrow. It seems that the music facilitated expression of my feelings about the entire illness experience. When I finished crying, I felt an enormous sense of relief, and slept very soundly that night.*[4]

To balance the stress, allowing respite for my body, mind, and soul, I have learned to relax deeply and experience comforting imagery, guided by music. Among my favorite musical selections are improvisations on classical themes, arranged and performed by Daniel Kobialka, including *Fragrances of a Dream, Going Home*, and *Timeless Motion*. You will find two selections of Kobialka's music on the CD that accompanies our book. Living with chronic health challenges has allowed me to learn meaningful life lessons. I embrace my human condition, focus on capability, and reach out to you with music.

FROM OUR EXPERIENCES

We have learned our lessons well. Our experiences in managing our own struggles have inspired us as professional music therapists. We offer you the most successful clinical strategies that we, and our colleagues, have tested in numerous research experiments. In this book, we help you find the music that is right for you, and show you how to implement and adapt techniques to suit your needs. We hope that you will find these music methods effective in handling your own life's challenges.

---

[4] Mandel, 110.

PART I:
THE FOUNDATION

CHAPTER 1

What Can Music Do for You?

Thoughts spin and collide
My muscles spark in friction
Music brings the balm

—Suzanne B. Hanser

Perhaps you have been plagued with stress and pain for much of your life. You may have carried this burden with you for as long as you can remember. Take heart! The caterpillar carries its weight for a long time, and cocoons itself, before transforming into a symbol of lightness and beauty: the butterfly. If you can work through your weighty difficulties and lift yourself above them, the victory may sustain you through new challenges. The more you cope, the more you learn that you can cope! To live is to struggle, and through struggle you may develop a broadened perspective on life and an enhanced appreciation for beauty and happiness.

We also know that even the simplest difficulty can get out of hand and create gigantic problems. As music therapists, we use intensive clinical strategies to assess and address these concerns. We have found that our clients are able to implement many music techniques on their own to manage their distress and to continue their trajectory of improvement. We have collected the most effective of these music programs in this book. Your success in applying these methods to your own unique needs is contingent upon a number of factors, some under your control, and others not at all. However, we know that if you are able to make music more a part of your life, you will benefit.

Our book is designed to help you manage and maintain a positive and creative approach to your challenges. We want to help you maximize your creativity and enjoyment of music through tried-and-true music strategies. These techniques are based on research studies supporting their effectiveness with people who have experienced everyday stresses and strains, life-threatening illnesses, and much in between.

OUR MUSIC THERAPY RESEARCH

Our personal experiences led us to discover music therapy methods that helped us cope with our own stress and pain. The impact was so positive that each of us wondered whether others could benefit as much as we did from using music for personal wellness. We began to introduce our strategies into clinical practice with clients who had a wide variety of needs and experiences. When we realized that these music therapy interventions were, indeed, very successful with the majority of our clients, we determined to conduct research that would identify and document the precise effects of the music techniques. Here are some of the research findings that inspired us to write this book.

CHILDBIRTH

As described in the introduction to our book, Suzanne's experience in childbirth was a dramatic testament to the ability of music to manage pain. To determine whether listening to music could help women with less complicated labors, Suzanne collaborated with Sharon Larson and Audree O'Connell, two qualified music therapists and colleagues at University of the Pacific.[1] They recruited seven participants for a research study by visiting prepared childbirth classes in the Stockton, California community, and met with each pregnant woman who volunteered, along with her coach. They interviewed each couple about the music that:

1. had a positive impact on their moods

2. elicited pleasant memories

3. was slow and relaxing

4. was rhythmic and attention getting.

Then one of the researchers observed each pregnant woman in the woman's home, as she listened to segments of her preferred music to confirm that it had the predicted effect. The investigators compiled lists of the selected songs and music in order of gradually increasing tempo, carefully identifying the specific track she needed.

---

[1] S. B. Hanser, S. C. Larson, and A. S. O'Connell, "The Effect of Music on Relaxation of Expectant Mothers during Labor." *Journal of Music Therapy* 20, no. 2 (1983): 50–58.

When one of the participants went into labor, she called her obstetrician and her music therapist, and one of the therapists accompanied her into the labor room. The very slow and relaxing songs that also brought up pleasant memories were used primarily in the beginning stages of labor. As contractions became more intense and frequent, more rhythmic and faster music was used, as the woman was encouraged to breathe along with the music. Of course, she could choose the particular selection she desired at any point. Later, during the transition phase, the investigators introduced the most rhythmic and attention-getting music. Always, they valued her choice of music over any of our recommended selections.

They wanted to evaluate the degree of pain that each participant experienced while she listened to her specially selected music compared to what she experienced without it. As researchers, they needed a basis for comparison, so they played the music for ten contractions and then, turned it off for the next five, played it for the next ten, followed it with the next five off, and so on, throughout labor. During each contraction, they observed the woman's reactions relative to pain by noting whether she showed tension in her body (flexed feet, gritting teeth, shoulders hunched, fists, eyes shut tightly), shifted her position in bed, requested medication, or vocalized pain. (We'll let your imagination provide some of these examples.) They compared her pain responses during contractions when music was playing to those during contractions when her music was not on. Every subject showed fewer pain responses when her music was present.

DEPRESSION AND ANXIETY

Some years later, Suzanne earned a National Research Service Award grant from the National Institute on Aging (NIA) to test the impact of music therapy on older adults who had serious depression. This postdoctoral fellowship allowed her to work at Stanford University Medical School and the Menlo Park Veterans Affairs Medical Center with the esteemed Dr. Larry Thompson, codirector of the Older Adult Research and Resource Center.[2] The NIA was interested in a stress-reduction strategy that was cost-effective and accessible to people who were homebound, either because they were ill themselves or were caring for a sick or disabled loved one at home. The people who participated in this research were over the

[2] S. B. Hanser, and L.W. Thompson, "Effects of a Music Therapy Strategy on Depressed Older Adults," *Journal of Gerontology* 49, no. 6 (1994): 265–269.

age of sixty, clinically depressed, and anxious. Many were taking care of a family member with dementia, and several were grief stricken from the loss of a spouse. She came up with eight music listening techniques that required them to identify music that was important to them and to listen regularly, while performing certain activities designed to reduce stress. All participants were randomly assigned to one of three experimental conditions, in order to evaluate the relative effectiveness of the music program: ten people learned these techniques individually in a weekly home visit; ten learned them from written instructions (that you will find in part II of this book) and a weekly check-in phone call; and ten constituted a control group and were placed on a waiting list to participate as soon as their part in the research was completed, but were not yet given music therapy techniques.

All of the participants who learned and practiced the music listening techniques reduced their depression and anxiety, and enhanced their self-esteem and mood, over the eight-week research period. Their improvement in depression was so great that it was "clinically significant." This means that, while these older adults were clinically depressed at the start of the music therapy program, by the end of the eight weeks, their scores on a test of depression more closely resembled a sample of older people who were not depressed. Those who participated in the music conditions scored significantly better than the control group, according to statistical analyses. Furthermore, all of the positive changes recorded on standardized psychological tests were maintained over nine months following the end of treatment.

CANCER

More recently, Suzanne served as music therapist at the Zakim Center for Integrative Therapies at Dana-Farber Cancer Institute in Boston. There, a team of colleagues in various specialties, including music therapy, oncology medicine, nursing, and research, came together to examine how music therapy could affect the quality of life of women who have metastatic breast cancer.[3] They recruited seventy women undergoing chemotherapy to participate in this study. Half of them met with Suzanne or music therapist Lorrie Kubicek during three of their outpatient chemotherapy treatments; half were randomly assigned to a control condition without music therapy.

[3] S. B. Hanser et al., "Effects of a Music Therapy Intervention on Quality of Life and Distress in Women with Metastatic Breast Cancer," *Journal of the Society for Integrative Oncology* 5, no. 1 (2006): 14–23.

The first music therapy session was similar to the music listening sessions of earlier research experiments, only this time, the music therapists provided live music for stress reduction. In the second session, they started with live music that the participant enjoyed most, and then, invited her to improvise along with the therapists. They provided percussion instruments that could be mastered without much instruction, including drums and instruments from around the world for a rhythm section, hand chimes and xylophones for creating melodies, and a dulcimer for harmonic accompaniment. In the third session, they invited each patient to compose songs on any subject. With help from the therapists, some wrote songs for or about their loved ones, some wrote about their experience with their illness, and some wrote about how music helped them cope.

Before and after each session, the researchers measured each participant's blood pressure and heart rate to test her stress arousal. They found that blood pressure was quite variable amongst this group of women, and they were unable to take a reliable reading on many of our participants because the women were being infused with chemotherapy during music therapy. But the subjects' heart rates decreased significantly from start to finish of the music therapy session. The investigators also asked each woman to rate her comfort, happiness, and relaxation. The participants reported significant improvement in all of these dimensions, demonstrating that the music therapy sessions made a difference, physiologically and psychologically. Although long-term changes were not apparent, the women's reactions to music therapy were overwhelmingly positive, with a majority of participants reporting great relaxation through music as an important outcome.

CARDIAC ILLNESS

You probably know someone who is living with cardiac disease, or perhaps you've had concerns about your own heart condition. Do you realize that ongoing stress, like continuous worry about money, can affect your heart health? Because chronic stress can put a person at risk for developing heart disease, Susan, Suzanne, and colleagues decided to study how participation in a music therapy program affected anxiety, stress, and blood pressure of people who were undergoing cardiac rehabilitation at Lake Health, a healthcare system in Ohio.[4] Susan

[4] S. E. Mandel et al., "Effects of Music Therapy on Health-Related Outcomes in Cardiac Rehabilitation: A Randomized Controlled Trial," *Journal of Music Therapy* 44, no. 3 (2007): 176–197.

conducted the music therapy sessions. First the group discussed how they were coping with stress. Then they listened to live and recorded music of their choice, sometimes accompanying it with musical instruments. At the end of each group meeting, the participants reported how the music activities affected their stress.

Each participant brought home a personalized music-assisted relaxation and imagery (MARI) recording. Susan developed MARI to help the listener counteract negative effects of chronic stress by relaxing with music recorded along with Susan's verbal guidance. Each individual MARI recording interspersed Susan's spoken suggestions to relax the body and mind with instrumental music recorded by Daniel Kobialka.[5] Kobialka's recordings were selected because they incorporate properties of music that research suggests to be conducive to relaxation, including slow tempo, soft dynamics, and long phrases. Susan blended her vocal suggestions with the music, just as a vocalist combines her singing with the sounds of the orchestra. Personalized MARI recordings included verbal introduction of relaxation techniques, such as deep breathing and guided relaxation, along with suggested thoughts and images to promote relaxation, comfort, and healing, based on individual needs. These techniques are described in part II of this book, and examples are included in the accompanying CD (tracks 11 and 15). In addition, an example of Kobialka's music is also included without verbal suggestions (track 16).

Through this study with patients who have heart disease, Susan and Suzanne learned that the people who participated in at least three music therapy sessions along with cardiac rehabilitation experienced significantly more improvement in systolic blood pressure, anxiety, and stress than those who only attended cardiac rehabilitation.

In order to better understand the impact of music therapy, Susan, Suzanne, and colleagues decided to study eight new patients more extensively.[6] These cardiac rehabilitation participants listened to a pre-recorded MARI CD[7] at home, without participation in a music therapy group. Those who enjoyed the pre-recorded music and vocal suggestions and listened regularly for at least three months improved in their systolic blood pressure, as well as anxiety and stress.

---

[5] For more information on Daniel Kobialka's music, visit www.wonderofsound.com

[6] S. E. Mandel, S. B. Hanser, and L. J. Ryan, "Effects of a Music-Assisted Relaxation and Imagery Compact Disc Recording on Health-Related Outcomes in Cardiac Rehabilitation," *Music Therapy Perspectives* 28, no. 1 (2010): 11–21.

[7] D. Kobialka, and S. E. Mandel, *Harmony of Mind & Body: A MARI Experience* (LiSem Enterprises, 2005), 108.

RESEARCH UNDERWAY

Just as many people have heart disease, many are also living with diabetes. In fact, diabetes has become a worldwide epidemic. Susan is now investigating how music therapy and listening to a pre-recorded MARI CD can influence the health of people with diabetes mellitus. Participants in the study are assigned to one of three groups: diabetes self-management training (DSMT) only, DSMT plus independent listening to the MARI CD, or DSMT plus participation in group music therapy sessions. Blood sugar, blood pressure, stress, and anxiety are being measured to compare changes in health after three months. Because the research study is currently in process, results are not yet available.

Meanwhile, Suzanne has been evaluating the applications of music strategies with people who have dementia (the confusion often associated with Alzheimer's disease) and are living at home with their family caregivers.[8] In this case, the person with dementia and the caregiver are listening to music together, using many of the techniques you will learn in this book. In this research, the caregivers, speaking for themselves and their loved ones with dementia, have reported similar changes in comfort, happiness, and relaxation to the women with cancer in Suzanne's previous investigation. The caregivers also expressed enthusiasm for the techniques that enabled them to reminisce together with their loved ones, enhance their time together, and expand their repertoire of positive, shared experiences.

END NOTE

We have devoted our careers to helping many individuals cope with stress and pain, using music as therapy. We will introduce some of these remarkable people to you through the following chapters. We hope that you are inspired by our words and music, as well as by the example of others, to use our techniques to manage your stress and pain through music.

[8] S. B. Hanser et al., "Home-based Music Strategies with Individuals Who Have Dementia and their Family Caregivers," pending publication.

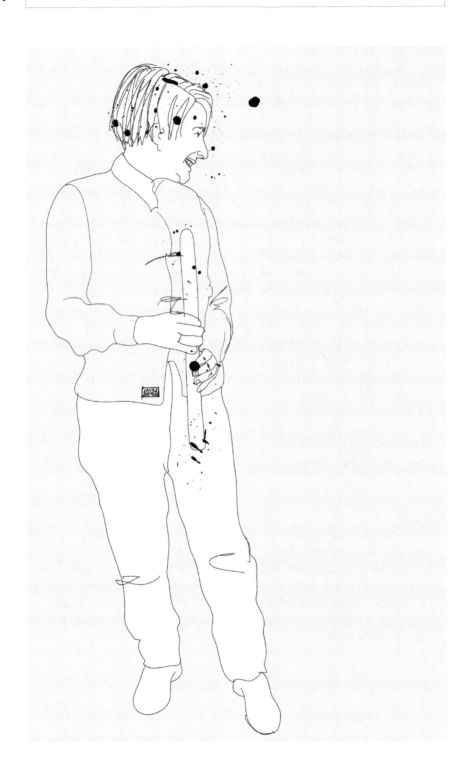

CHAPTER 2

What Is Stress?

I sing soprano
High above earthly traffic
Finding harmony

—Suzanne B. Hanser

Long ago, daily life used to be dangerous—in fact, under constant threat. Early humans encountered wild beasts at any turn in their paths. Fortunately, they became effective hunters, adept at using simple tools as weapons to kill their prey. But truly, their survival was due to the ability of their bodies to react quickly—automatically—to the sighting of a threatening creature. As soon as they recognized that an animal posed a potential threat, their sympathetic nervous systems (SNS) switched right on. This resulted in immediate, adaptive physiological changes. Their hearts raced, their blood pressure shot up, and the blood drained from their digestive systems to feed their muscles. This prepared human beings for two things: fight or flight. Enhanced circulation allowed them to fight back with greater strength. If they realized that their efforts were futile, faster heartbeats and heightened blood pressure oxygenated their bodies, giving them vital energy needed to run away with vigor.

So humans not only survived, they also evolved into the mammals that we are today. We have larger brains, upright postures, and less hair, but our sympathetic nervous systems still react to threat in the very same way. Only, contemporary threats have changed: too many e-mails, too much traffic, and more tasks to do than we have time in the day are typical of the stressors in our modern world. Perhaps you have more than your share. Maybe that's why you picked up this book. Our longer life spans enable us to worry about our parents as well as our children, and this great quantity of days does not always bring great quality of life. The American Heart Association cites stress as a contributing factor for heart disease[1], and stress is implicated in almost every other life-threatening illness.

We suffer the demands all around us with concern in our heads and anguish in our hearts. Meanwhile, our sympathetic nervous systems work overtime to cope with threat after threat, stress after stress, day after day. The SNS signals our hearts to pump more strenuously with each stressful event, eventually weakening the heart and straining the rest of our other major organs. Now, this once life-saving part of our nervous systems is, ironically, responsible for putting us at risk for disease and death. You are probably aware that stress is running your life, but you may not have known that it could be killing you.

Stress is a broad, colloquial term that you probably know well. Stress is also a complex process that affects, and is affected by, multiple factors. Stress itself can be defined in many ways; a more technical term is *allostatic load*. Allostasis describes the process that our bodies go through as they seek to maintain balance, or homeostasis, while our behavior, physiology, and environment are changing.[2] Homeostasis is that balanced state of being that is also referred to as equilibrium. Our endocrine, nervous, immune, and neurological systems are jostled about in this process of allostasis until they achieve stability, or homeostasis. As you can imagine, this ebb and flow of changes in our bodies and brains can strain the delicate balance of the systems that keep us alive. When allostasis progresses well, a stressor activates an appropriate response, like elevated blood pressure, that may be sustained for a while, but then turns off or returns to normal. Allostatic *load*, however, refers to the consequences endured by the body when the stress response fails to turn off or regulate, due to too much stress or a faulty stress response schema. Allostatic load also results when we believe we have insufficient coping resources for dealing with the demands on us. And so the stress response lingers and taxes our bodies.

Another way to look at stress is in psychological terms. *Eustress* is also known as good stress, versus *distress*, which is bad stress. So, the stress felt by the orchestral player, who works hard to express the composer's intentions while keeping up a swift tempo, is probably *eustress*, a condition that holds some positive benefits. Alternatively, the stress that causes generalized anxiety before the concert is *distress*, which may result in a poor performance. This roller coaster of emotion is evident as we encounter other types of environmental requirements.

[1] American Heart Association, "Risk Factors and Coronary Heart Disease," www.americanheart.org/presenter.jhtml?identifier=4726.

[2] P. Sterling, and J. Eyer, "Allostasis: A New Paradigm to Explain Arousal Pathology," In *Handbook of Life Stress, Cognition and Health*, eds. S. Fisher and J. Reason (New York: John Wiley & Sons, 1988).

Yet, whatever the combination of eustress and distress, the body does not discriminate. All types of stress tax our bodies, making us work hard to fight whatever threat our minds have conjured up. Even a successful performance will exhaust the player, who may emerge from the stage perspired and out of breath.

Some would say that any triumphant performance demands stress—that the performer must be pushed with a burst of noradrenaline to achieve the most magnificent sounds and original musical interpretation. Noradrenaline (or norepinephrine) is a neurotransmitter that facilitates connections between the neurons, or cells in our brains. But noradrenaline is also a stress hormone—a chemical released from our adrenal glands that pumps us up when the SNS activates. As such, it is responsible for accelerating our heart rate, directing the blood to flow into our muscles, and causing a myriad of other bodily functions to prepare us for lifesaving action. Some performers count on this tension to catapult them into a new level of super awareness or peak experience.

Abraham Maslow (1970) introduced the term *peak experience* as a sense of unity, ecstasy, joy, or awe. He likened it to the creative wonder or spiritual understanding that occurs when achieving the highest form of human need, self-actualization. Clearly, creating, playing, singing, or listening to music are all capable of evoking such a condition, when the musical elements converge to produce a deeply moving experience.

The peak experience is also part of the breakout principle described by Harvard Medical School professor, Herbert Benson.[3] The breakout principle involves four stages that lead up to the height of creativity, performance, or insight: struggling with a stressor, feeling a release, engaging in a breakout or peak experience, and discovering a new state of body and mind. In the example of the musical performer, playing the music leading up to a musical climax is the work that the player engages in. Right before this peak in the music, there is a release, and then comes this awesome moment when the orchestra comes together in perfect resonance and harmony. When Benson and colleagues studied this phenomenon,[4] they learned that the chemical compound nitric oxide (not to be confused with the nitrous oxide that you may have inhaled at the dentist's office) was released just before the peak experience. What is amazing is that *nitric oxide* counteracts the effects of stress hormones, like norepinephrine. So perhaps the musician who experiences eustress and an associated peak experience is actually

[3] H. Benson, W. Proctor, *The Breakout Principle* (New York: Scribner, 2003).

[4] G. B. Stefano et al., "The Placebo Effect and the Relaxation Response: Neural Processes and Their Coupling to Constitutive Nitric Oxide," *Brain Research Reviews* 35, (2001): 1–19.

achieving homeostasis through the interaction of norepinephrine and nitric oxide. This musician also leaves the stage aglow in the unearthing of an enhanced and self-actualized state of mind and body.

At the other end of the spectrum, too much stress is hazardous to your health. Do you ever get sick after a stressful period? We do. When we are doing too much, when we worry about too many people, or when we sense that there are just not enough hours in the day, we are at risk for disease. That's because, in its valiant journey to homeostasis through allostasis, the body engages the help of the immune system. When we are under chronic stress, our natural survival mechanisms are constantly running to restore balance to the body. This unstable allostatic load weakens our bodies' defenses against infection and our immune systems in general. Much research has identified the crosscurrents between the nervous, endocrine, and immune systems, and we are still uncovering more interactions between the chemicals that facilitate brain activity and the health and wellness of our bodies.

Back in the nervous system, there is another important way to counteract the shock of SNS activity. There is actually a complementary set of processes generated in the parasympathetic nervous system (PNS) that has the opposite effect. The PNS decreases heart and breathing rate, blood pressure, circulation, and arousal. It sends the neurotransmitter acetylcholine coursing through the brain. The outcome is rest and relaxation, a palliative measure for the harmful physiological and emotional reactions to stress.

How can we turn on the PNS when we are bombarded with assaults from the SNS? Once again, we have Dr. Herbert Benson to thank for a way to improve our health by relieving symptoms of stress and thus, warding off the myriad of diseases that evolve from chronic stress. Benson's landmark book, *The Relaxation Response* (1975), tells us how to do this by meditating, breathing, and finding ways to relax. There is also evidence that passive music listening and guided imagery to music are effective techniques in the music therapist's toolbox to elicit a deeply restful condition, and in some cases, an altered state of consciousness or sense of profound peace.

Humorist Loretta LaRoche points out that the word "stressed" is just "desserts" spelled backwards. Perhaps she has the right idea. If we could frame our stressed lives as just desserts that we have earned from millions of years of human struggle, it might put all those traffic jams into perspective.

CHAPTER 3

What Is Pain?

Pain can serve a purpose
Cause you to attend
To your own condition
Allowing you to mend

Balance is the key
To manage the pain you feel
Learn lessons as you grow
Find comfort as you heal

Stress is part of life
Helps you to do your best
Or to deal with danger
Followed by a rest

Balance is the key
To manage the stress you know
Relief in relaxation
Quality of life is the goal

—Susan E. Mandel

Pain—who needs it? A pain in the neck, a pain in the behind, the royal pain at the office. Pain can be irritating or debilitating. Just like stress, it is a companion to most of us at least some of the time. And just like stress, pain can be your enemy. But pain also has its adaptive functions designed to help you survive.

Pain trips the alarm that tells you to get away from the flame. It signals you that something is wrong with your body, and you had better do something about it. You can remove the splinter or retreat from the stove, but unfortunately, pain is often more insidious and elusive. Your headache creeps up on you. You don't know why or what to do about it. Your back pain makes you moan with a gnawing sensation that seems to eat into your bones. Your achy muscles warn you to stop overdoing it.

Pain can ruin an otherwise pleasant day. Most of us consider pain to be a nuisance. Somehow we learn to live with the discomfort and get on with our lives.

There are many types of pain. Some pain is acute. The sudden bruise or fall causes pain, but you know it is going to dull over time and you will recover. When you undergo a medical procedure, you expect to have some pain, but you know it will stop when the doctor or nurse is finished. When pain is short-term and predictable, you have to cope with the shock of its brief impact. Your perceived pain is as dependent upon your history with pain and on your prediction of how you will feel after the painful event as the assault itself. You see, pain is a personal phenomenon.

According to Suzanne:

> You and I may both be pricked by a needle in the same parts of the skin, but I may howl in dismay while you claim not to have felt a thing. Pain is a perception and completely individualistic. My pain is no more real than yours, nor yours more than mine. The distinguishing characteristics are our own unique ways of experiencing and managing it. The good news is that, because this invisible thing called pain is your own perception, you can change the way you perceive it, and in the process, actually feel pain differently.

Let's look at how complex that example can be. Suzanne enters the laboratory for a blood test, and she is thinking, "Oh no, I have no tolerance for pain and always find the needle unbearable." As soon as she says, "Oh no," she is setting up an expectation for a negative experience, and that self-fulfilling prophesy may, indeed, become true. If her previous blood draws were quite painful in the past, she will likely predict a similar outcome the next time she needs to have a blood sample taken. Her dread alone is contributing to a tightening of her muscles. It is that tension that may be the primary reason for the insult to her skin to feel so painful. If she believes that she has "no tolerance for pain," then that belief may affect her reaction more than the sight of the needle itself.

When Suzanne looks at her own history, she sees that there are circumstances that she can control in order to make the ordeal easier.

> *I recall that during my last blood test, the nurse didn't warn me about when the needle would pierce my skin. I even thought the nurse took some joy in watching my blood fill the vial. Next time, I will ask for an account of exactly what will happen and when, or I might ask for a different nurse. I realize that it was just my last blood test that was so uncomfortable. Other tests have not been as bad.*

This realization challenges her thought that she always finds the needle unbearable, and she brings a new attitude to the following tests. She might recognize that her fear that the results will reveal some horrible diagnosis may be the underlying cause of her distress. Picturing the needle might conjure up horror film scenes that she has watched with terror.

This analysis shows that there might be what is known as a *secondary gain* to Suzanne's fears.

> *If I make a fuss about going for a blood test, perhaps my girlfriend will accompany me (and we'll go shopping afterwards). That's a lot of reinforcement for my angst. In fact, all of these conditions—my fears, memories, previous experiences, beliefs about pain, imagining the needle, and rewards for my anxiety—determine my pain response. Then, the pain that is so nebulous and uncontrollable becomes something I can begin to understand and manage.*

Just thinking about a blood test might set your heart racing and your memory bank depositing scary images all over this page. Alternatively, you may not relate at all to Suzanne's experience.

If you deal with chronic pain, then you know that taking control of your pain is neither simple nor clear-cut. Chronic pain is something that you live with constantly. If you suffer from conditions for which medical treatment is largely ineffective, like migraine or arthritis, your pain may flare up repeatedly and unexpectedly. The ebb and flow of chronic pain may make it appear more uncontrollable than acute pain because it is unpredictable. Having experienced the pain before, you know what is coming and how awful it can be. It is easy to give up trying to cope when your pain has gone on and on.

The same factors that affect the perception of acute pain may be in play with chronic pain. Severity and nature of the pain are, obviously, implicated. The added distress of a long-term condition can also result in depression or anxiety, and sometimes, a sense of helplessness. When you feel at the mercy of your pain, you give it the power to rule your life.

Sometimes Susan's back aches, just like you may have experienced at one time or another. But because she has undergone many spine surgeries, her anxiety is quickly aroused by her awareness of back pain. Her thoughts race: "What's wrong now? Is another surgery approaching? How am I going to deal with another interruption of my life? Maybe my back aches because I have been sitting in my desk chair for hours, writing this book." But anyone's back could ache with prolonged sitting in one position.

> *All I need to do is get up, take a few deep breaths, and walk around for a few minutes before returning to work. If I allow negative thoughts to continue, the pain will likely increase along with my anxiety. I need to stop and check it out. Each time my back pain resolves without surgery, I recognize that not all pain is equal. And therefore, I have learned to moderate my response to pain by changing my thought patterns. The more I cope with pain, the more I learn that I can cope through pain. This belief in my own ability to manage pain is a self-fulfilling prophecy.*

No matter how you experience pain, this example is intended to demonstrate that you can influence how you perceive pain and learn to manage it. In short, if you can change the way you *feel about* pain, you can change the way you *feel* pain.

We have focused on the perception of physical pain, and have introduced some factors that may affect your pain. Despite major advances in medical technology and know-how, pain management still poses great treatment challenges. One reason for this is the complexity of the mechanisms that affect pain. We hope that, by providing some explanations for how pain is processed, you will be convinced that you can take control of your pain.

Pain follows certain pathways from body to brain, then from brain to body, and back and forth, all in an instant. One path, the neospinothalamic, is for sharp pain, and the other, the paleospinothalamic, for more dull or throbbing pain. When your body's tissues are damaged, pain signals move up the spine, one way or the other, into the brain stem. There, two structures, the medulla and pons, are called into action. The medulla tracks these signals, and the pons relays messages to the thalamus in the brain's limbic system. The thalamus then spreads these signals out to the hypothalamus in the limbic system, the cortex, and other parts of the brain. The "Gate Control Theory of Pain"[1] describes how pain impulses travel up through the dorsal horn of the spinal cord, while other pathways that inhibit pain are descending from the brain down the spinal cord into the body. This is due to the cortex sending out messages that constrain the brain's interpretation of the pain signal. Melzack and Wall postulated that a gate opens or closes at the dorsal horn, and this is where the descending signals that modulate pain can prevail over the ascending pain signals. Updating his gate control theory, Melzack (2001) devised a neuromatrix theory to explain the multidimensional nature of pain that acknowledges such diverse elements as one's background, thinking, stressors, immune system, emotion, and sensory stimulation. Just as in the mechanisms of stress described in chapter 1, neurotransmitters play a significant role in changing how you feel pain.

The neurotransmitters released in the dorsal horn include opioid peptides, endorphins, and norepinephrine (remember those in our discussion of stress?). When these chemicals connect with opioid receptors on the neurons of the dorsal horn, pain is not transmitted very effectively. These outcomes open the way to control pain by changing the conditions surrounding pain impulses.

Mind-body approaches, including music therapy, provide sensory stimulation, competing thoughts, and mood changes that result in the release of opioid peptides directly. Herein lies a key to how you can take control of pain and manage your response to it through music. When you focus on music and engage with it actively, your mind may be engulfed in images, memories, and associations that bring about a positive outlook. When you identify your own special music, you can even improve the impact of music on your mind, body and spirit. You can learn to discriminate between music that relaxes you deeply and music that grabs your attention. You can see how certain music focuses

[1] Melzack, R., & Wall, P.D., "Pain Mechanisms: A New Theory," *Science* 150 (1965): 971–979.

your concentration and distracts you from pain. With practice, you can become aware of just how music is affecting you, and how you can change the music to change how you feel.

We recommend that you seek professional consultation for your particular symptoms. If you are in pain, a physician may be able to determine the physical basis for your distress. The delicate balance of endocrine and hormone functions may be upset by physical abnormalities that are causing you to feel pain and/or stress. If this is the case, medical intervention is indicated in order to help you to feel better. If pain or stress are interfering with your functioning at home or on the job, visiting a psychotherapist or other mental health professional is also advisable. There may be particular treatments that are necessary to control your unique symptoms. Your pain or stress may also be warning signs of problems that require other forms of therapy. Seeking help from those who can observe and diagnose your specific issues is always a good idea.

CHAPTER 4

Assess Your Needs

Alone in the void
Echoes of my voice tell me
Everything I need

—Suzanne B. Hanser

Self-assessment helps you comprehend what is going on when you are under stress or in pain. It can also help you determine what you need from music. By asking yourself some simple questions, you can evaluate how you feel, and then test the impact of certain music.

Dr. Albert Schweitzer, a Nobel prize–winning physician, believed that you know yourself better than anyone else. He said, "Every patient carries her or his own doctor inside." Taking a little time to appraise what is happening in your body and mind when you are in discomfort may also help you to identify the appropriate action for you. If your stress or pain requires a medical intervention, we recommend that you consult with professionals, explore diverse approaches, and pursue treatment. You are responsible for your own healthcare.

You may choose to respond to our suggestions by writing in the provided log sheets (see appendix B for larger versions), writing in a journal, or keeping a record on your computer or PDA. If writing is not your style, we certainly don't want to increase your stress by asking you to write. But we suggest that you take time to think about the ideas we present in this chapter and see how they resonate with your own experience. However you choose to proceed, we believe that music can help supplement or complement other pain and stress management methods.

THE NATURE OF YOUR STRESS

When do you feel stress? Is it only when you are under pressure to meet a deadline or are stuck in traffic? Does it happen at certain times of day, or when you enter your office, car, or home? Do you feel stress around particular people? Does stress keep you from sleeping?

Take an entire day to notice when you are under stress. Then, the next day, observe whether the same patterns recur, or new sources of stress become apparent. What happens before and after you feel stress?

If you are the type of person who keeps a journal or likes to write things down, a daily log may help you describe the nature of your stress and also keep track of your progress. The following is a Stress Assessment Log, a version of which is located in appendix B of this book that will be easier to photocopy. Feel free to make multiple copies of the log in appendix B to track your stress over multiple days. If you take notes as we suggest, you may find clues that will help you predict upcoming stress. When you see the signals coming, you can be prepared to head them off, cope with them, or avoid them completely.

Stress Assessment Log
Rating Scale

| 0 | 1 | 2 | 3 | 4 | 5 |

0 = No Stress   5 = Most Stress

Date 1:_____   Date 2:_____

Describe your stress   **Stress Rating**

List stressful events   Date 1   Date 2

1. _____   _____   _____
2. _____   _____   _____
3. _____   _____   _____
4. _____   _____   _____
5. _____   _____   _____
6. _____   _____   _____

Describe how you feel tension in your body.

Rate your bodily tension.

	Date 1	Date 2		Date 1	Date 2
• Head and Face	_____	_____	• Muscles (central)	_____	_____
• Neck	_____	_____	• Legs	_____	_____
• Hands	_____	_____	• Knees	_____	_____
• Arms	_____	_____	• Feet and Ankles	_____	_____
• Shoulders	_____	_____	• Other	_____	_____
• Back	_____	_____			

Describe your thoughts.

Stressful Events   Date 1 Thoughts   Date 2 Thoughts

1. _____   _____   _____
   _____   _____   _____
2. _____   _____   _____
   _____   _____   _____
3. _____   _____   _____
   _____   _____   _____
4. _____   _____   _____
   _____   _____   _____
5. _____   _____   _____
   _____   _____   _____
6. _____   _____   _____
   _____   _____   _____

Fig. 4.1. Stress Assessment Log

First, write down the instances when you feel stress. For each of those instances, think about the severity of your stress, and give it a rating. Use a simple scale of 0 to 5, where 0 is no stress, 1 is very little stress, 3 is moderate stress, and 5 is the most stress you can imagine feeling. Keeping track of your ratings as you recheck your stress will also help you see your progress in managing your stress.

The following is an example of a stress rating for a patient we'll call Max.

Date 1: _10/12_		Date 2: _10/13_
Describe your stress		**Stress Rating**
List stressful events	Date 1	Date 2
1. *Waking up late and rushing off to work*	3	4
2. *Co-worker tells me she is nervous about new supervisor*	2	
3. *Feeling really hungry, but having too much work to do*	2	
4. *Leaving a little late, and catching a lot of traffic*	3	
5. *Arriving home to an angry spouse because I'm late again*	4	
6. *Argument with spouse over dinner*		5

Fig. 4.2. Example Stress Assessment Log: Events

As you can see, Max is experiencing stress from morning through evening. There are lots of triggers for feeling stress, one of which, "Waking up late and rushing off to work," occurs two days in a row. On the second day, when Max rechecks stressful events, there is an argument over dinner that results in the most stressful rating.

What happens when you feel stress? Are you feeling stress now? If so, you can continue by asking yourself some questions. If not, the next time you are feeling stress, take a few minutes to notice what is happening.

WHAT DO YOU FEEL IN YOUR BODY?

In this body assessment, you will move distinct parts of your body very gently. Be sure that you don't strain your body when you move as suggested. The instructions are meant to call your attention to areas of discomfort outside of your general awareness. As you go through each movement, notice how your body feels. If a movement hurts you, stop doing it. If you experience pain during this self-assessment, please consult with your medical advisor to rule out problems that may not necessarily be stress related.

- Open your mouth wide. Look up and stretch your eyebrows. Do you feel any tension in your jaw or face?

- Take your fingertips to your forehead and scalp. Are you locating tender areas?

- Turn your head slowly from side to side and then make circular motions of your head around your neck. Do you feel any tight spots?

- Make fists with your hands, and then spread your fingers. Do you experience any sensitivity in your hands?

- Bend your forearms from your elbows, up and back. Do you feel stiffness?

- Reach out with your hands and circle your body with your arms. Do you feel any tension in your shoulders?

- Lift your shoulders up towards your ears, and then release them back down. Make gentle circles with your shoulders. Do you hear a pop or feel discomfort in your shoulders or back?

- Twist your body right and left from your waist. Does that strain your muscles in an uncomfortable way?

- Lift each leg straight in front of you. (If you are standing, hold onto something as you do this to keep your balance.) Is there any tension in the joints or pain in your legs?

- Bend your knees. Do you feel any discomfort?

- Point your toes and make circular movements around your ankles. Are you feeling tightness in your feet or ankles?

- Scan your whole body once more by identifying any areas where you noted tension. The next time you feel stress, go through these movements again, and see if you are experiencing discomfort in the same parts of your body. Repeat the assessment as often as you wish to monitor where and how stress is affecting your body.

If you like to keep notes, go back to the Stress Assessment Log, and check the places in your body where you feel tension related to stress. Find a time of day when you tend to feel stress, and note on the log where you are experiencing tension, along with its severity. Use the scale of 0 to 5 again, only this time, 0 is no tension, 1 is very little tension, 3 is moderate tension, and 5 is the most tension you can imagine feeling. You may locate what can be thought of as an Achilles' heel—a particularly vulnerable area where tension resides during times of stress. Here is another example from Max's Stress Assessment Log:

	Date 1	Date 2		Date 1	Date 2
• Head and Face	3	3	• Muscles (central)	0	1
• Neck	4	5	• Legs	0	0
• Hands	0	0	• Knees	0	0
• Arms	2	2	• Feet and Ankles	0	0
• Shoulders	3	4	• Other	0	0
• Back	3	3			

Fig. 4.3. Example Stress Assessment Log: Body Assessment

Max commented:

I feel tightness in my neck when I am rushing to work and back home. Once I became more self-aware, I notice this same neck tension each time my wife and I argue.

WHAT IS GOING ON IN YOUR MIND?

When you feel stress, what are you thinking? Do you tend to worry? Do you think the worst? Are you hard on yourself, using words like "I should have," or "I did it again," or "Why didn't I?" Do you see things in the extreme, like "I can't ever get it right," or "She always makes me mad?" Do you imagine the future to be bleak? Is your mind so flooded with thoughts that you can't think clearly?

Hopefully, you don't recognize yourself in these examples. But if you do, you can help yourself. Writing down your thoughts when you are under stress can be instructive. When you see them on paper, it is easier to look at them from a more objective and less emotional view, and you can begin to decipher patterns in your thinking. You can also see how destructive your thoughts can be. In *The Feeling Good Handbook*,[1] Dr. David Burns offers several examples of how negative thinking and beliefs can result in depression and anxiety. Burns' cognitive approach reveals that you can feel better when you challenge dysfunctional thoughts that get in the way of more positive and constructive feelings and actions.

Do you recall the song "Anything You Can Do" from *Annie Get Your Gun*? Frank cries, "No you can't, can't, can't," and Annie insists, "Yes I can, can, can." This refrain echoes the idea of replacing negative thoughts with positive ones.

The next time you feel stress, write down all of the thoughts that are going through your head. See if you fall into the habit of thinking negative thoughts. Then note the emotions that you are feeling, and see if you can find the connection between your thinking and feeling.

Max reveals negative thoughts and feelings in the following example from the Stress Assessment Log:

---

[1] D. D. Burns, *The Feeling Good Handbook* (New York: Plume, 1999).

Describe your thoughts.

Stressful Events	Date 1 Thoughts	Date 2 Thoughts
1. *Awake Late*	*Oh no. I'm going to be late. I've done it again. I'll be fired.*	
2. *Nervous co-worker*	*I'm worrying about this and I can't get my work done.*	
3. *Hungry*	*I feel edgy. I want to eat. I need to get my work done.*	*If I don't get this done I'll get fired.*
4. *Leaving late*	*I HATE traffic. Why can't I get out earlier?*	*I'm doomed to leave late, be stuck in this blasted traffic.*
5. *Angry spouse*	*I work so hard. I'm tired. I'm never good enough. I hate my life.*	*Now I'm really in for it. I can't keep going on this way.*
6. *Argument*	*I'm always in an argument. I should be a better person. Why can't I get my act together?*	

Fig. 4.4. Example Stress Assessment Log: Thoughts

Can you see how feeling "doomed" to repeat self-defeating behavior impedes chances of getting "my act together?" Do you remember the children's book, *The Little Engine That Could* by Watty Piper? By repeating "I think I can, I think I can…," that little engine chugged over the mountain and realized, "I knew I could." The little engine story demonstrates the impact of positive thoughts. When you develop a personal music plan, you can learn to replace negative thinking with beautiful music and affirming song lyrics that encourage your own positive thoughts.

THE NATURE OF YOUR PAIN

Are you ever in pain? Pain does seem to be a part of most of our lives. Where do you feel your pain? Is it a chronic and ongoing ache or does it act up every now and then? If you take time to identify and describe your pain, it may assist you in discovering what you need to help you to cope with the discomfort. Please also discuss your pain with your healthcare provider to rule out serious conditions that may require medical attention.

You may choose to use the Pain Assessment Log that follows, which is also found in appendix B.

Pain Assessment Log
Rating Scale

```
|----+----+----+----+----+----|
0    1    2    3    4    5
```

0 = No Pain   5 = Worst Pain

Part 1: Rate your bodily pain.   Date: _____

	Pain Rating			Pain Rating
• Head and Face	_____		• Muscles (central)	_____
• Neck	_____		• Legs	_____
• Hands	_____		• Knees	_____
• Arms	_____		• Feet and Ankles	_____
• Shoulders	_____		• Other	_____
• Back	_____			

Part 2: Describe your pain

- Constant or intermittent
- Cold or hot
- Other

- Sharp or dull
- Focused in one area or diffused

_____

_____

_____

_____

Part 3: How and when does your pain change?

- During and after activities (walking, exercising, singing, etc.)   During   After

_____   _____   _____

_____   _____   _____

_____   _____   _____

- During and after quiet times (reading, music listening, etc.)   During   After

_____   _____   _____

_____   _____   _____

_____   _____   _____

- Other distractions   During   After

_____   _____   _____

_____   _____   _____

_____   _____   _____

Part 4: What increases and what eases your pain?

_____

_____

_____

_____

Fig. 4.5. Pain Assessment Log

We suggest that you make multiple copies of the blank Pain Assessment Log for your continued use. Begin by rating your pain. Use a simple scale of 0 to 5, where 0 is no pain, 1 is very little pain, 3 is moderate pain, and 5 is the most pain you can imagine feeling. Then think of descriptive words that express your pain in a few sentences.

You may find it helpful to see how Alexa, a patient with jaw pain, rated and described what she was feeling.

Part 1: Rate your bodily pain.   Date: _____

	Pain Rating		Pain Rating
• Head and Face	*4*	• Muscles (central)	*0*
• Neck	*4*	• Legs	*0*
• Hands	*1*	• Knees	*0*
• Arms	*2*	• Feet and Ankles	*0*
• Shoulders		• Other	*5*
• Back	*1*		

Part 2: Describe your pain
- • Constant or intermittent
- • Cold or hot
- • Other

    • Sharp or dull
    • Focused in one area or diffused

The pain in my jaw is burning and sharp. It spreads into my neck, the back of my head, and down into my shoulders. The pain makes it hard to concentrate at work and often wakes me up at night.

Fig. 4.6. Example Pain Assessment Log: Rating and Descriptions

Pay attention when you notice your pain changing. Is your pain different when you engage in passive activities like reading or listening to music? What happens when you participate actively in walking, exercising, or singing? What changes occur when you have your mind on other things? Write down your impressions of your pain and how it is affected by different activities.

Alexa noticed the following changes in her jaw pain during and after activities.

Part 3: How and when does your pain change?

	During	After
• During and after activities (walking, exercising, singing, etc.)		
When I sit at my computer at work, the pain seems to get worse the longer I am there.	*4*	*4*
When I walk out of doors and pay attention to the sights and sounds around me,		
I don't seem to notice as much pain.	*2*	*3*
• During and after quiet times (reading, music listening, etc.)	During	After
When I listen to my favorite music (country western) and sing along with the words of	*1*	*1*
the songs, I seem to forget about the pain.		

Fig. 4.7. Example Pain Assessment Log: Changes

Is there any activity that tends to decrease your pain? What makes it worse? Write in your Pain Assessment Log on several different days of the week, and notice how your pain changes. Remember to make several copies of the blank log sheet. You may begin to see a relationship between your activities and your pain level. If so, you can try to decrease or discontinue those activities that increase your pain. If that is not possible, perhaps you can adjust your daily routine to include more of the things that increase your comfort.

After several days of self-observation, Alexa wrote the following in her pain assessment log:

> *I notice that my jaw pain increases at work. I know that my work is very stressful to me, but I can't afford to quit. I see that when I take a walk, listen to music, or sing along, my pain eases. So I started taking a walk during my lunch hour, and I am listening to music at night before I go to sleep. Though my jaw still aches at work, I'm learning that I can manage the pain. I'm beginning to wonder if I clench my jaw when I feel stressed.*

YOUR PERSONAL MUSIC

Has music ever made you cry? Does it remind you of special times or special people? Is there a song that gives you the chills? Perhaps you sing in prayer at religious services and feel a sense of unity with the congregation. The car radio may make your commute seem a little shorter. You might realize that the music playing in the background in the restaurant makes your meal taste a little better. Sometimes there is something magical about how music moves us. But music is more than magic. Empirical research has demonstrated how music can be applied successfully to cope with stress or pain.

If you've ever listened to a piece of music that pulls memories from long ago right back into the present, or evokes emotions like love, joy, or longing, then you know firsthand how music has the power to change your experience of stress and pain. There is music that uncovers beautiful places in your past, and music that is capable of inspiring an optimistic future. If you have found some music that has changed your mood just a bit, then we can help you find the music to manage the stress that upsets and the pain that hurts you. If the idea of allowing music to influence your stress or pain is new to you, our book provides an opportunity to explore new possibilities.

This book is about finding comfort through music—listening to it, creating it, and singing or playing it. We "play" music; we don't "work" music. When you play music, you engage in an ongoing process of choosing and reacting to the sounds being produced. Whether it's an instrument or a recording, you select what you wish to play, based on your needs at that moment. In an instant, you may feel changed—your memories, associations, and expectations of the music may evoke an emotional response, and you feel different. As the music continues and changes its tune, your attention to it may help you to be "in the moment." As you remain present with yourself and the music, you may become aware of changes you are experiencing as a function of the music. Music may transport you. It may be possible to leave your distress behind as music beckons you to find a place of beauty and calm. Worries about the future may dissipate when you are concentrating on the experience of music. You may even discover a feeling of playfulness that eases your stress and pain, however unlikely that might seem right now.

Sometimes just experiencing some favorite music takes you away from your troubles. It may just turn you on, or change your mood without your giving it a thought. It may bring you back to a meaningful time in your life, or trigger a memory of an exceptional place or person. It might make you think of where you were and how you felt when you first heard it. The music could give you goose bumps, or induce a state of calm, without your awareness of what is happening. Noticing how music affects you will tip you off to its potential to change how you feel when you need it most.

What Music Will You Choose?

Now that you have assessed your problems, it is time to choose the music that will help you manage stress and pain. To take an inventory of your musical preferences, begin by listing some recordings that you like (or just add them to your portable music device). You may then find it helpful to make note of your music listening experiences. If you do, take a look at the Music Listening Log that follows, and is also located in appendix B.

Music Listening Log

Rating Scale

```
|----+----+----+----+----|
0    1    2    3    4    5
0 = None              5 = Most
```

Date: _____

Playlists (categories)
A. *Attention focusing*
B. *Energizing*
C. *Relaxing*
D. *Sleep inducing*
E. *Spiritual*
F. *Other* _____
G. *Leftovers*

Favorite Music Selections:

• **Music with happy memories**

	Rate Relaxation	Rate Enjoyment	Playlist
Childhood _____	____	____	____
	____	____	____
Teenage years _____	____	____	____
	____	____	____
Television, movies, concerts _____	____	____	____
	____	____	____
Relationships _____	____	____	____
	____	____	____
Milestones, celebrations _____	____	____	____
	____	____	____
Vacations _____	____	____	____
	____	____	____
Religious or spiritual occasions ____	____	____	____
	____	____	____

• Recent listening_____

____	____	____
____	____	____
____	____	____
____	____	____

Match Your Music

	Playlist		Playlist
Good morning	____	*Painful encounters*	____
Off to work	____	*Bedtime*	____
Household chores	____	*Weekends*	____
Time to unwind	____	*Travel*	____
Stressful moments	____	*Other*	____

Fig. 4.8. Music Listening Log

Perhaps you already have a music collection. That's a great start. Now think of music that has special meaning to you. In childhood, were there songs that your family sang? Were your teenage years a good time of your life? If so, what music was popular? Were there songs from television shows, movies, or concerts that were memorable? What music was played at your first dance or with your first love? (You decide whether to include these!) What music do you associate with milestone events, celebrations, or vacations? Is there spiritual or religious music that is important to you? Write down or download all of those selections that played a positive role in your history.

After you have strolled down memory lane and recalled the names of those songs and music, focus on your more recent listening habits. What, if any, music do you enjoy in the morning? Do you listen while traveling? During the day, are there pieces that keep you going or affect your mood? Do you listen to music at the end of the day?

Once you have collected this music, play each selection and listen attentively to the effect it has on you. This process may take a while, but you can listen to one piece each day or just pay a little more attention when listening to the music. See what you notice and rate your relaxation as well as the enjoyment of your experience with each selection. You may use that now familiar scale, with 0 representing no relaxation or enjoyment and 5 indicating the most relaxation or enjoyment you can experience.

Next, you can categorize these choices into playlists that suggest certain outcomes for you. Here are some potential groupings:

A. **Attention-focusing** music has a strong rhythm or significant lyrics that catch your attention. Music that brings out your most vivid and positive images or memories may be indicated here. This music may be most likely to provide a distraction from unpleasant tasks, pain, or anxiety, when you feel at your worst.

B. **Energizing music** peps you up or induces a happier mood. This may be the music to play when you are tired or can't seem to get started on something.

C. **Relaxing music** lets you forget your worries and reminds you of something familiar and comforting. This music may be capable of soothing you when you are stressed.

D. **Sleep-inducing music** often leads you to deep relaxation or a pleasant doze. It may be challenging to find this music. Not everyone can fall asleep to music, so you may choose to dispense with this category.

E. **Spiritual music** transcends your usual reality. Some music causes chills or goose bumps, or evokes a sense of peace or awe. It defies description. If music has this effect on you, you can count on this music for hope or faith when you need it most.

As you divide your selections into playlists or create some mixes for different moods or purposes, you will undoubtedly find music that fits more than one category. You may also identify music that fits none at all. Keep these leftovers in a category of their own, and don't forget them. When you're not sure what you need, these extra pieces may fill the bill. When you listen to them again, see what you discover.

Go ahead and plan when you want to listen to your playlists or mixes. You might wish to have music for morning listening to set a mood for the day. You could select music to play when you return home from a busy time, or to relax you while doing chores or preparing a meal. You might designate some music to play before anticipated stressful events. You may also wish to create a category of music to listen to during potentially painful events, like a medical or dental procedure.

The following is an example from the Music Listening Log of a patient we call Lynette. Notice how Lynette was able to identify music to help her cope with different experiences, as noted at the bottom of her log.

Favorite Music Selections:

	Rate Relaxation	Rate Enjoyment	Playlist
● **Music with happy memories**			
Childhood _____			
When You Wish Upon a Star	4	4	C
Teenage years _____			
Staying Alive	0	3	B
Television, movies, concerts _____			
Sound of Music	3	4	A
Relationships _____			
Sunrise, Sunset	4	4	A
Milestones, celebrations _____			
Silent Night	5	5	C, E
Vacations _____			
Copacabana	0	4	B
Religious or spiritual occasions _____			
Amazing Grace	5	5	C, D, E
Recent listening _____			
Defying Gravity	0	4	A, B

Match Your Music

	Playlist		Playlist
Good morning	B	_Painful encounters_	A, E
Off to work		_Bedtime_	
Household chores	A, B	_Weekends_	
Time to unwind		_Travel_	
Stressful moments	C, E	_Other_	

Fig. 4.9. Example Music Listening Log

AN EVOLVING PLAN FOR MUSIC

Once you have identified your all-time favorites, listen to some music you have never heard before, and assess what it does for you. You could listen to a new radio station, download some samples from an online digital media store such as iTunes, or tune into some tracks from the CD included with this book. Unfamiliar music offers the novelty of new discoveries and surprises that can take your mood into new directions. We urge you to try it.

Commit to a realistic plan to engage in the music programs we describe in part II. We recommend that you sample each technique, continue to practice those that appeal to you, and feel free to reject ideas that don't fit your needs or lifestyle. Certain strategies work better for some people than for others. As you read, we encourage you to make note of the programs that resonate with you and ameliorate your stress or pain. We hope that you will be able to adapt the music programs to meet your unique needs and desires, as you encounter new challenges in your life.

We created the Music Plan Worksheet that follows (see appendix B for a version that you can photocopy) to help you to think about your response to the various programs that are introduced in part II of this book, and to develop your personal music plan. Again, feel free to make copies of the blank form so that you can use the worksheet as often as you choose.

Music Plan Worksheet
Rating Scale

```
|-------|-------|-------|-------|-------|
0       1       2       3       4       5
```

0 = None   5 = Most

Date: _____

Program	Musical Selection	Relaxation	Enjoyment
• *Take a Deep Breath*	_____	_____	_____
• *A Musical Workout*	_____	_____	_____
• *Musical Massage*	_____	_____	_____
• *Building a Bond with Music*	_____	_____	_____
• *Finding Inner Harmony*	_____	_____	_____
• *Sensing Peaceful Images*	_____	_____	_____
• *Discovering Your Imagination*	_____	_____	_____
• *Focus Your Attention*	_____	_____	_____
• *Creative Problem Solving*	_____	_____	_____
• *Lullaby and Good Night*	_____	_____	_____
• *A Musical Boost*	_____	_____	_____
• *Singing*	_____	_____	_____
• *Chanting*	_____	_____	_____
• *Songwriting*	_____	_____	_____
• *Playing an Instrument*	_____	_____	_____
• *Improvising*	_____	_____	_____
• *Silence*	_____	_____	_____

Which programs helped you to manage your stress or pain? _____

_____

_____

_____

_____

_____

_____

_____

_____

_____

_____

Fig. 4.10. Music Plan Worksheet

As you experience each of the programs that are described in part II, list the music selection to which you listened, and rate your relaxation and/or enjoyment. You will see the familiar rating scale at the top of the log, indicating that 0 means none and 5 means the most possible. After you experience the programs at least once—and preferably more often—take time to consider not only what was most helpful to you, but also what was not particularly helpful. After you have finished reading this book, think about how you propose to modify and continue your personal music plan.

You may find it interesting to review log entries from our patient named Tim.

Program	Musical Selection	Relaxation	Enjoyment
• *Take a Deep Breath*	Bach: Air on a G-String	4	4
• *A Musical Workout*	Abba: Dancing Queen	–	5
• *Musical Massage*	Sequioa (CD)	3	3
• *Building a Bond with Music*	Halpern: Spectrum Suite	3	3
• *Finding Inner Harmony*	(on CD)	4	4
• *Sensing Peaceful Images*	Ocean Sounds	3	4
• *Discovering Your Imagination*	(on CD)	4	4
• *Focus Your Attention*	Oklahoma	–	3
• *Creative Problem Solving*	Ocean Sounds	2	2
• *Lullaby and Good Night*	Ocean Sounds	5	4
• *A Musical Boost*	You Raise Me Up	–	5
• *Singing*	Do Re Mi	2	4
• *Chanting*	Ah	3	3
• *Songwriting*	My Favorite Things	3	5
• *Playing an Instrument*	Drum	2	3
• *Improvising*	Drum	2	3
• *Silence*	–	4	4

Fig. 4.11. Example Music Plan Worksheet

You will notice that Tim took time to experience each of the programs. He didn't appreciate "Creative Problem Solving," but really enjoyed "A Musical Workout," "A Musical Boost," and "Songwriting." "Lullaby and Good Night" was most relaxing to him while several other programs were relaxing as well. The following is Tim's response to the questions on the Music Plan Worksheet.

Which programs helped you to manage your stress or pain? _____

I discovered that I most enjoyed the music and activities that lifted my spirits. I found that music took my mind off my aches and pains. I liked the deep breathing and felt especially relaxed when I listened to ocean sounds that helped me to get to sleep at night.

Fig. 4.12. Example Music Plan Worksheet: Comments

Like Tim, you will likely discover that some programs are more effective than others in meeting your needs. That is to be expected. You may also find that some programs meet your current objectives, while others may be of help to you in the future. Furthermore, as you continue to experiment with selections, you will find the music that is most helpful to you. In fact, that is our point. We cannot offer you a prescription for specific music. You will want to consider not only your personal preferences, but also the concerns that you identified during your assessment process or recorded in the Stress Assessment and Pain Assessment Logs. As you read part II ("Create Your Personal Music Plan") of our book, you will have the opportunity to explore and experiment with music.

PART II:
Create Your Personal Music Plan

INTRODUCING YOUR PERSONAL MUSIC PLAN

Part II is designed to help you develop your personal music plan by providing a menu of music programs. We encourage you to experience each program with an open mind to possibility. When you dine at a smorgasbord, you may taste each selection to discover which foods are to your liking and meet your own dietary needs. In the same way, you will sample a variety of musical experiences through the programs described in this section. Soon you will discover what meets your needs and works best for you. In chapters 5, 6, and 7, you will learn how to master relaxation skills to help you feel better about yourself and the future. Simple activities guide you to relax while listening to different types of music. The music is intended to melt away tension and anxiety, as your mood shifts into a more positive state. The music programs are designed to help you develop a conditioned relaxation response to music. That is, with repeated listening, you begin to relax more quickly and easily every time you hear a particular piece of music. Then, when you are in distress, playing this music will more likely result in feeling comfortable and relaxed.

To maximize the benefit of these programs, we suggest that you find a time and place for daily practice, when and where you think you can be undisturbed. To protect your privacy, consider turning off the phone or doing whatever you can to facilitate a private practice session each day. It is best to find a time either prior to eating or more than an hour after eating when your body is no longer at work digesting the food. Try the activities during a coffee break at work, when you get home, or whenever and wherever you can steal a brief respite from the demands of your day. We strongly advise you to avoid experiencing the programs while you are driving a vehicle because they will distract your focus. We have learned that listening to each program at least two or three times enables you to familiarize yourself with the relaxation process. Your Stress Assessment and Pain Assessment Logs will help identify when to implement these music programs. Your Music Listening Log will assist you in identifying the best music selections to accompany each program. Use the Music Plan Worksheet to note the title of the music you choose for each program, and rate your relaxation and enjoyment. This will give you an indication of how well each music program worked for you, allowing you to plan future listening experiences when you really need to address your stress or pain.

The music programs in chapter 5 suggest that you concentrate on your body and breath. Chapter 6 helps you relax both your body and mind, guided at times by the music along with spoken voice. We also show you how to use comforting music to replace worries and dysfunctional ideas. Chapter 7 focuses on what is going on in your mind. Imagery exercises set the stage for thinking more clearly and solving problems while in a relaxed state. We invite you to experience a night's sleep with a musical lullaby, and at the other extreme, boost your energy with lively music. You are encouraged to play as much music as you like and to use or adapt the programs to suit your needs.

Passive music listening requires little more than choosing some music and pressing a button. If you're game, active music making can open a world of experience to transform your feelings. You don't need to have formal music training to play with music. Chapter 8 suggests adding singing and chanting to your day, while chapter 9 presents songwriting techniques to open your creativity and give the gift of song to others. Chapter 10 offers some ideas for expressing your feelings and releasing pain and stress through playing instruments and improvising. Chapter 11 explores the importance of silence in your life. Applications for various music techniques that help you cope with the benign stresses of everyday life are described in chapter 12. Chapter 13 shows examples of people dealing with pain and serious, ongoing stressors through music.

Although our book is about how you can use music to help you with stress and pain management, your creativity may guide you to experiment with diverse approaches to suit your particular needs. We encourage you to adapt and develop the ideas we express in your own unique way.

INTRODUCING YOU TO OUR MUSIC

We have filled the recording that accompanies our book with favorite selections from people who have benefitted from the music programs described here. We hope that you will appreciate this music when and where you need to relax, but you may also enjoy simply listening for pleasure. Of course, your musical taste is personal and unique, so we won't be offended if you don't find this music to your liking. But we would like to entice you to listen by telling you a little bit about our music.

The CD is designed to accompany the first seven music programs that are described in part II. "Take a Deep Breath" (track 1) is a set of suggestions that focus on the breath that gives you energy and life. It is followed by "Bonsai" (track 2), an original improvisation on hand chimes. We hope that the tinkling sounds of the chimes will facilitate a deeply relaxed state. "A Musical Workout" (track 3) recommends gentle movements that allow you to work out any body tension. It is followed by "Traumerai" (track 4), or "Reverie" in English, a popular piano piece by Robert Schumann from his *Scenes from Childhood*. This selection is meant to prompt flowing motions and a relaxed body. "A Musical Massage" (track 6) provides guidance on how to give yourself a gentle facial massage. "Sequoia" (track 7) is a musical improvisation on the Native American flute to accompany your massage. Next is "Building a Bond with Music" (track 8), with its directions for a progressive muscle relaxation exercise. To help you tense and relax each part of your body as part of this technique, we include "To a Wild Rose" (track 9) by Edward MacDowell and "La Fille aux Cheveaux de Lin" (track 10) by Claude Debussy, both performed on piano. "Finding Inner Harmony" (track 11) takes you through music-assisted relaxation with verbal guidance as you listen to Erik Satie's "Gymnopedie #1" from *Trois Gymnopedies* in a unique arrangement by our friend, Daniel Kobialka. "Sensing Peaceful Images" (track 12) guides you to a beautiful place in your mind's eye. "Clair de Lune" by Claude Debussy (track 13), performed on harp, helps to take you there. "Discovering Your Imagination" (track 15) is music-assisted imagery accompanied by Daniel Kobialka's "Lullaby." Track 16 is "Lullaby" alone, without the verbal guidance.

We hope that you enjoy the full compilation of music programs in part II. By first reading, then implementing them at your own discretion, you will discover your most helpful activities, and begin to design your own personal music plan.

CHAPTER 5

Body and Breath

worried-anxious-upset-stressed-concerned-fearful-angst-unrest
out of balance-mind askew-body trembles
what to do?
breathe in deeply and let down,
ease my mind, embrace unknown
welcome calm-allow release-renew trust-relaxed-free
need for worry?
wholly no
feel connection to let go
certain trust reflects in ease
soulful memory... re-found peace

—Susan E. Mandel

TAKE A DEEP BREATH

TRACK 1, 2

Prepare your music space; it is time for you! See if you can:
- set aside about half an hour when you can avoid disturbance
- find a comfortable place with good associations
- elevate your feet and settle into a position in which your body feels supported

If you find it difficult to find time to relax, recognize that in order to find the time, you need to believe that you deserve this opportunity to help yourself! Be kind to yourself. If your music time becomes another demand on you, then it won't be helpful. Set a reasonable goal. Can you find fifteen minutes? Five minutes? Start there. If your music time needs to be scheduled while you are preparing dinner, then go ahead and use that time. Consider scheduling the session before you go to sleep. The act of committing to a time and place just for you, even if it is brief and less convenient than you planned, is an important step to take. You may be incapable of modifying the pressures on yourself. But if you can take charge of a few minutes each day just for yourself, then you may be able to recognize and manage the pressures better. Taking control by making a small adjustment in your day can empower you to begin to change the way you approach those forces around yourself that seem uncontrollable. Acknowledge that your life holds stress and pain. Then for the moment, let those thoughts go, and get ready for music.

Sometimes it can be as simple as taking a few deep breaths. We are born knowing how to do that, yet somehow through the stresses of life, we often find ourselves holding our breath. You can train yourself to breathe deeply when you begin to feel stress and strain. Listening to a favorite piece of calming music can help you deepen your breathing rhythm. Often the music cues your breathing. You can find the slow, deep, even breaths in harmony with the music and in harmony with yourself.

Have you observed that when you pluck the string on a guitar, it vibrates? Do you notice that when the person in the automobile next to you blasts the radio at a very loud volume, your own car seems to shake? Just as music involves vibration, so our body systems vibrate. As music therapists, we use entrainment to help people synchronize their body rhythms to match rhythmic and other structural properties of music. Our colleagues, Cheryl Dileo and Joke Bradt, explain how music therapists first match music to a person's physiological rhythm and then gradually modify the music selection to evoke change in vibrational patterns of physiological responses.[1] Do you feel energized when you hear perky music, like a disco sound or a rock 'n' roll rhythm? If you pay attention, you may notice that your heart and breathing rates begin to quicken to catch up to the music's tempo. In the same way, your heart rate and breathing may slow down when you hear music that gradually decelerates. You can begin this process of entrainment by matching your deep breathing to the rhythm of relaxing music.

1. Find Relaxing Music

It may be familiar or unfamiliar, but the most important consideration is that you feel calm when you hear this music. A tempo of about sixty beats per minute is ideal because it matches an average resting heart rate. Many Baroque pieces of music, such as Bach's "Air on a G String," are played at about sixty beats a minute. Quiet music with long phrases and without sudden changes is likely to be relaxing to most people, but your personal preference will determine the most appropriate music for you. Experiment with different kinds of music included in

---

[1] C. Dileo, and J. Bradt, "Music Therapy in Stress Management" in *Principles and Practice of Stress Management* (3rd Ed.), ed. P. Lehrer, R. Woolfolk, and W. Sime, (New York: Guilford Press, 2007).

your Music Listening Log. You may also wish to play track 2 on the accompanying CD, an improvisation on hand chimes called "Bonsai." Verbal directions to guide you through "Take a Deep Breath" are found on track 1, and the music itself follows on track 2.

2. Breathe Deeply

Take a deep breath in through your nose. Slowly fill your belly with clean, refreshing air. As you breathe in, take in all that you need. When you are comfortably full, hold your breath just briefly. Then breathe out, and slowly release all that you no longer require. Each time you exhale, let go even more. When you breathe out, you may choose to repeat a sound—a simple syllable like "aaah," a word that has special meaning to you like "peace," or a phrase from a special prayer. When your mind wanders, as it probably will, gently bring your thoughts back to your breath and the music. Take some slow, deep, even, life-giving breaths along with the music. Let the music cue you when to breathe. Observe whether you are lifting your shoulders or tightening another part of your body while you are breathing. With the next breath, let the air enter your body while you check to ensure that your whole body is relaxed. When the music ends, take one more deep breath as you slowly bring your awareness to this moment. Notice how you feel.

3. Breathe with Your Music

You may wish to identify one special piece to accompany this deep breathing practice. After repeated listening, you may find that you begin to breathe deeply without conscious thought or effort, as soon as you hear the first few notes of the music. You may even learn to play the music in your mind when you want to calm yourself. If possible, remember some of the melodies and sing them to yourself when you need to relax.

4. Evaluate

Use the Music Plan Worksheet to note the title of the music and its effectiveness in helping you relax. Do you feel differently than you did before you heard the music? Observe what is going on in your body and your mind. How does your body feel? What are you thinking?

Describe your mood. Make any notes that will assist you in adapting this program for future use. Is there another piece of music that you would like to try next time? Is there another time of day when you think this music program will be helpful?

We hope that "Take a Deep Breath" has helped you find the power of your breath and your music. We believe that when you feel more relaxed, you can see yourself with greater perspective and openness. When you are more yourself, you are more capable of identifying your resources and personal strengths. With those assets, you can face your stressors and your pain with more clarity. With practice, you can become more and more adept at locating that inner strength and feeding it with life-affirming breath.

A MUSICAL WORKOUT

TRACK 3-5

"A Musical Workout" is designed to have you locate and work out any body tension that you might have. It is a gentle exercise set to music to help you convert this tension into relaxed, flowing movements. It may be particularly useful when you feel agitated or cannot sit still. It may also be appropriate when you are in pain, as long as movement is not contra-indicated by your doctor. Even when you feel comfortable, it still helps you recognize spots in your body that may be holding tension without your awareness. Be sure that you only move your body in ways that feel good. If you have any conditions that affect your mobility, consult your physician before proceeding.

Examine your Stress Assessment and Pain Assessment Logs. Where have you felt body tension in the past? Pay attention to those parts of your body where you tend to feel stress or pain. This workout is designed to remind you to work out the kinks in those vulnerable areas.

1. Find Some Special Music

Identify some of your favorite music. Choose music that is energetic, peppy, or just makes you feel good. It might have a solid, strong beat, but it could also flow sweetly in lovely, long phrases. It can be of any style, and it might be vocal or instrumental. Most importantly, well-chosen music will bring to mind positive associations and good feelings.

Refer to your Music Listening Log. Is there some dance music amongst your favorites? Find the most rhythmic pieces, and play these while you follow the instructions below. Were you able to add energizing music to your playlist? You can also try the second musical selection on our accompanying CD, a classical piano piece by Robert Schumann, entitled "Traumerai." You may listen to verbal instructions on tracks 3 and 5, and "Traumerai" on track 4.

2. Breathe Deeply

Sit upright or stand as you listen to the first sounds of the music. Take a deep breath in through your nose. Exhale through your mouth. Fill your belly with a deep breath, and then let it out. Release any tension or worries with your exhalation. Take in another full breath, and let your abdomen expand. Feel the energy it brings into your whole body. Breathe deeply as you listen, letting the musical phrases tell you when to breathe. Notice your even and rhythmic breaths. As the air enters the center of your body, let it expand your abdomen and feed you what you need. Exhale with the sound of "aaah" to release everything you don't require right now.

3. Move Easily

Shift your position until you feel balanced and centered, with your weight equally distributed between the right and left side of your body. Begin to sway gently and move your arms from side to side, guided by the music. Start to move quietly, and gradually add energy to each movement until the musical phrase comes to an end. Move only in ways that are comfortable for you. Move your head in slow circles as you identify any tension in your neck. Draw circles with one shoulder, reverse direction, and circle the other shoulder. Are you breathing deeply? How does your body feel?

4. Find a Way to Move

Keep the movements as light and flowing as the music. Each time you hear a new melody, find a new way to act out the music. Use your toes, legs, hips, head, shoulders, elbows, wrists—but never force or jerk your movements abruptly. Try circular, side to side, and up and down motions. Repeat the movements that feel good. Let the music guide you, coming to rest at the end of each phrase.

5. Feel Balanced and Centered

Check your breathing, making sure it is slow and rhythmic. Assess your balance to make sure you feel secure. Experience what it feels like to be centered. Take a deep breath, slow your movements, and come to rest, as the music comes to an end.

Stand up and repeat the process with more music, challenging your creativity to find new ways to move your body. Move a part of your body that you didn't move before. Move your straight arms through space, then bend them every which way and swing them around. Move fast and slow, light and heavy, directly and in twisting movements. Move and bend your legs in different directions. Feel your weight shift gently as you point your toes and then, bend them back to flex your feet. When the music stops, be sure that you feel balanced and centered. Take a deep breath, and exhale "aaah" through your mouth. Take note of any changes your body feels right now.

6. Dance

If you have no restrictions regarding mobility or flexibility, use this listening time to dance along to your favorite music. Dancing is a natural response to music that moves you. Create your own unique dance. Go with the music. It will inspire you, and your body will find ways to interpret the music. As you create this dance, focus on moving one part of your body at a time so that you can pay attention to how your dance affects your body. Start with your head, lifting it regally as you glide across the room. Circle your shoulders in one direction and then another, as you work out any kinks. Let your arms dance in free movements that remind you of flying, floating, or whatever image makes you feel light. Twist your middle body gently from side to side. Bend your knees and make your body into a new shape. Let the music move you. Let the music excite you. Let the music dance you around.

Gradually slow down. As the music ends, gradually slow your movements to wind down and come to a rest. Take a deep breath, exhale, and observe how different your body feels.

7. Move On

Use the Music Plan Worksheet to note how effective "A Musical Workout" has been for you. If you enjoyed this exercise, try it again with different music that sets a positive mood. Try some new dance steps as you step up the pace with music of a faster tempo. Try a new style of dance music. Ballroom? Hip-hop? Ballet? Better yet, enroll in a dance class of your choice. Join a yoga studio, and learn to link your body, mind, and spirit. There are all sorts of movement strategies, from Pilates to Feldenkrais. Check your local listings for classes near you. Befriend your body as your favorite music inspires and moves you.

A MUSICAL MASSAGE

TRACK 6, 7

When you are upset or depressed, you may not be aware that you are walking around with a scowl on your face, knitting your brows in concentration, or tightening the muscles around your face. When you look angry or tense, others may be less inclined to smile at you or start a conversation. It is easy for this cycle of events to intensify your feelings of sadness, depression, loneliness, or isolation. In order to reverse this spiral of bad feelings, you can start by recognizing when you are experiencing facial tension.

One unpleasant symptom of facial tension is a headache. The stresses in your life can cause headaches that recur and become resistant to treatment. This program deals with such problems in the head and face. If these exercises are effective for you, try them on other parts of the body where your muscles feel tense.

"A Musical Massage" is designed to make you more aware of tense muscles in your face. It enhances your listening experience with a gentle facial massage accompanied by one of your favorite musical selections. This program may be especially helpful if you have a headache or tend to clench your jaw, grind your teeth, or strain your face in other ways. Check your Stress Assessment and Pain Assessment to identify where you tend to feel tension or pain. While this exercise suggests that you focus on your head and face, you can also direct your massage to any part of your body within reach.

1. Find Your Special Music

We recommend familiar and calming music for this program. It can be vocal or instrumental, but well-chosen music will bring to mind good associations and a pleasant mood. Select some of your favorite music from your Music Listening Log. Try out those selections in your relaxing music playlist. We also offer you "Sequoia," played on the Native American flute (track 7), along with verbal directions on track 6.

2. Locate Tension

As the music begins, locate any tense parts of your face. Do you have a headache? Do you feel tightness in your jaw? Use your fingertips in a small, circular motion at your temples, then under your cheekbones and behind your jaw, while you check for tension around your face. Take your time, discovering and exploring the many facial muscles you have. Before continuing, exercise any tight areas by stretching them slowly and carefully. If this causes you more discomfort, stop and rest while you focus on the soothing elements of the music.

Open your mouth gradually, becoming aware of any tension in your jaw. Smile, frown, pucker, and move your mouth in as many ways as you can, all the while working out muscle tension. Let your mouth relax in a comfortable position. Open and close your eyes, slowly and carefully, while your fingers gently surround your eye sockets and travel back toward the temples. Raise your eyebrows and look up, left, down, and right, as you canvas the room and notice colors, shapes, and familiar objects.

3. Soothe with Massage

When you are ready to continue, start at the top of your head with a gentle scalp massage. Use the entire musical phrase to massage this area with an extremely light, comfortable pressure. Work your way down your face with fingertip circles. When the next phrase begins, concentrate on your forehead, moving gradually from the temples to the center of your face. Gently manipulate your eyebrows, cheeks, and jaw, taking a full musical phrase to knead the skin around each area of your face.

4. Pinch Lightly

Use both index fingers to lightly pinch the top of your nose, working down the bridge to the base of your nose while pressing softly in small circles. Pinch your ear lobes and outer ear quietly, so as not to interfere with the music.

5. Treat Your Body

Work your way down into your neck, where you can palpate areas of tension to loosen any knots you find. Only massage places that feel good, and use the amount of firmness that feels right. You may wish to move into your shoulders, lower back, or other areas of your body, using the finger pressure that feels best. When you have done enough, start at the top of your head and repeat the process to see if you can feel any changes in spots that were previously tense. Emphasize problematic areas of your body, and use the massage to give yourself some tender, loving care. If you like, give yourself a hug. Embrace your body; it is all yours! If you have time, administer the Stress Assessment again, and see how differently you feel.

6. Evaluate

Use the Music Plan Worksheet to note your response to "A Musical Massage." Next time you try this program, you will have a better idea of the most fitting musical accompaniments.

7. Touch

Consider getting a massage from a professional. There are also somatic therapies that concentrate on working through your body's responses to pain, stress, or trauma. If you pursue practices that work on your body, be sure to bring along a portable music device to complement your treatment.

BUILDING A BOND WITH MUSIC

TRACKS
8–10

"Building a Bond with Music" is a progressive muscle relaxation (PMR) exercise accompanied by music. PMR is a standard relaxation technique, developed by Edmond Jacobson, which involves tensing and releasing sets of muscles throughout the body. We can learn to relax by first perceiving the difference between tensing and relaxing parts of the body. The performance of this technique is greatly facilitated when the pulse of accompanying music imitates the tension/release that you are exerting. After repeated practice of this technique, it is possible to feel deeply relaxed when you hear just a few measures of the music. As a word of caution, if tensing any part of your body causes you pain, then just imagine tightening those muscles and allow yourself to release the tension there.

Once you have found music that works well for you, we suggest playing that music repeatedly for this program. After you complete the exercise, continue listening to this music in order to appreciate the effects of the music while you enjoy a respite from the concerns of the day. We remind you that scheduling time for you and your music is an important aspect of this method. Set a realistic time period and see if you can remain uninterrupted a little longer than usual. Better yet, find a second time of day for a brief music refresher.

When you are nervous about an upcoming meeting, appointment, other stressful event, try this program, or a part of it. If you have difficulty falling asleep, try it before bedtime. When your body is relaxed, you may find yourself drifting off to sleep.

1. Find Your Special Music

The background music for this program is slow, melodious, and pleasant. We recommend instrumental music or songs without words. You might enjoy string music with this, perhaps played on the guitar, harp, violin, or cello. Avoid music with abrupt changes. See if you can find music that flows in long phrases. Many ambient compositions that are designed to serve as unobtrusive, background music fit these criteria. But the most helpful music will be selections that you like and find calming. Check your relaxing music playlist from your

Music Listening Log to see if any of your special music meets these requirements. We invite you to listen to the verbal instructions for this exercise (track 8) followed by two short piano pieces: "To a Wild Rose," by Edward MacDowell (track 9) and "La Fille aux Cheveux de Lin," by Claude Debussy (track 10).

2. Breathe with the Music

Close your eyes and rest your body in a comfortable chair or bed. When the music begins, let your entire body become heavy and relaxed. Inhale with a deep, cleansing breath; exhale and let any tension leave your body. Breathe with the music—deeply, easily, and slowly. Now with each musical phrase, you will tense and relax a different part of your body.

3. Check for Tension

Gently roll your head around your neck, never forcing any movement. Become aware of any tension in your neck and let the weight of your head guide you in a circular path, as you notice and release any tense areas. Circle your head in the other direction, slowly and carefully. Let your head rest comfortably on your shoulders.

4. Lift and Roll

Lift your shoulders up toward your ears, hold, and then carefully roll them back and around, working out any tension in your shoulders. Lift your shoulders again. Then, rest them in a comfortable position, as the melody resolves and also comes to rest. Do the same in the opposite direction. Next, lift your arms in front of your body, one at a time, clenching your fists. Feel the tightness. Hold each arm straight briefly, and then let each arm relax and fall heavily into a comfortable position.

5. Relax and Breathe in Rhythm

Tighten your middle body, contract your stomach muscles, and inhale deeply. Hold the tension briefly. Then exhale, letting all your weight rest comfortably in the chair. Tighten your middle body again and then release. Next, straighten your legs, one at a time, and feel how tight the muscles are. Hold each leg straight briefly, and then let your leg relax and fall heavily into a restful position. Your legs are more heavy and relaxed, you are breathing to the music, and feeling calmer with every note. Let the gentle rhythm of the music continue to regulate your breathing.

6. Tense and Relax

At the start of the next phrase, flex your feet one at a time. Feel the tension in each foot, hold the tension briefly, and then release it, moving your foot in gentle circles. Gradually, let your feet come to rest in a comfortable position, feeling more heavy and relaxed. Your head, shoulders, arms, middle body, legs, and feet are more heavy and relaxed than before.

7. Relax

Gently scan your body. Locate any part of your body that feels uncomfortable or tense. Tighten that area and then relax. Move gently or shift your position slightly until you feel even more relaxed. Breathe with the music, releasing tension with each breath, and enjoy its beauty. The more times you listen, the easier you will find it to achieve a deeply relaxed state.

8. Evaluate

Use the Music Plan Worksheet to note how effective "Building a Bond with Music" has been for you. If you are using this program to fall asleep, make your notes immediately when you arise on the following morning. You can also add the number of hours you slept or how restful the night was, after listening to the music. This will let you know whether the music is helping you sleep.

9. Feel the Difference

Once you really feel the difference between your tense muscles and relaxed ones, you will be in a better position to identify when your body is reacting to stress in a dysfunctional manner. Given the insidious way that tension creeps up on our bodies and attacks us while we are attending to other things, checking in and noticing that tight shoulder or crick in the neck may help you avoid more serious physical consequences, like headaches and backaches. When you do locate those areas of strain, you will know just what to do, and what music to play. Add this progressive muscle relaxation technique to your compendium of methods to connect your body and breath with your very special music.

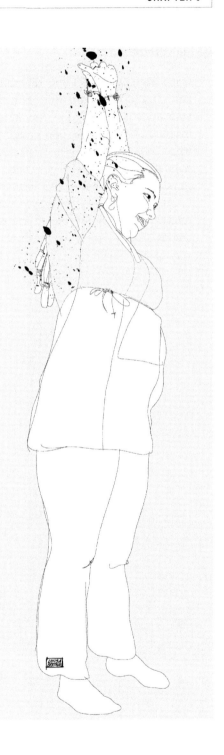

CHAPTER 6

Relax Your
Body and Mind

Wind's steady hum brushes the leaves,
Rhythmic water laps,
Trucks' bass drone intermittently sounds.
Grow more still—to listen.

Dishes' raucous clank,
Leaves' steady shake,
Crescendo and quiet.
To listen.

Splash... walk... children talk...
Metrical symphony.
Quiet within, heart rate still,
Peaceful and calm.
To listen.

—Susan E. Mandel

FINDING INNER HARMONY

TRACK 11

If you were able to practice the music programs described in the last chapter, you are now familiar with how deep breathing and progressive muscle relaxation may help you relax while listening to your own preferred, calming music. The program located on track 11 of our accompanying CD blends verbally guided relaxation with music that Susan has applied in her research. This program is based on music-assisted relaxation and imagery (MARI), which she developed to help patients who have heart disease cope with stress. Daniel Kobialka's recording of "Gymnopedie #1" from Eric Satie's *Trois Gymnopedies* is the musical partner for her words. The combined experience of listening to the verbal instructions along with the music is intended to help you relax both your body and your mind.

1. Listen

Trust yourself to experience what you need when you listen to this selection. Sit or lie down in a comfortable place where you will not be disturbed. A word of caution: please do not listen to this program while driving an automobile or operating equipment. It is intended to help you relax deeply. There are no messages imbedded in the music, so there is no need for concern about subliminal suggestions. You will consciously hear and process all of the recorded information while you remain fully in control of your response. If you are interrupted unexpectedly during your listening experience, take a few deep breaths before you return to the music.

2. Evaluate

Use the Music Plan Worksheet to note how effective "Finding Inner Harmony" is for you over time. Many people have found that they benefit most from listening to the recorded program when they play it daily for several weeks. Your response to the music and your schedule will determine when and how often you choose to listen.

3. Repeat and Adapt

After regular practice, you may choose to apply this technique with your own relaxing music from your Music Listening Log. You will find another selection of Daniel Kobialka's music included on track 16 of our accompanying CD. This lovely "Lullaby" may bring you into a state of deep relaxation on its own.

SENSING PEACEFUL IMAGES

TRACKS
12–14

"Sensing Peaceful Images" provides a way of relaxing your mind. It involves a guided imagery exercise that lets the music fill your mind with pleasant and calming images. Some of the most suitable music for evoking beautiful imagery is inspired by nature. The rhythm of the galloping horse, the staccato touch of rainfall, and the swift flowing movement of a brook are examples of easily recognizable musical techniques composers use to emulate sounds of nature. By changing the tempo, rhythm, dynamics, orchestration, and other elements of music, composers are able to mimic familiar sounds in creative ways.

Some music has become associated with specific pictures in the mind's eye. *The William Tell Overture* is unmistakably paired with an image of the Lone Ranger for people who heard the radio or television program. Music played at a time of joy or sadness often evokes those moods, even many years later. Certain associations may be very strong, and yet, outside of our consciousness.

Even though many people sense similar images when listening to a piece of music, your imagination is unique to you and you alone. In this program, you will see where the music guides you. We hope you find that your music helps relax and clear your mind of unwanted thoughts and feelings in the process.

1. Use Caution

If you have a history of difficulty controlling your emotions, or a psychiatric condition, do not engage in the "Sensing Peaceful Images" program without professional assistance. In the unlikely event that you experience troubling images or emotions, just open your eyes and breathe deeply until you feel calmer. If your discomfort persists, we advise you to seek professional help.

2. Draw Pictures in Your Mind

For some people, imagery comes quickly and naturally while listening to music. Perhaps you have never experienced pictures in your mind when you close your eyes. Be assured that you are still capable of enjoying deep relaxation. In fact, sometimes the music releases a flood of memories and emotions. Sometimes it simply changes your mood. As you may not be able to predict your response to this music program, it would be helpful to have someone you trust available to debrief your first listening experiences. Before you begin, see if a friend or family member will be online, free to talk, or even better, able to listen with you.

Some music therapists use a psychotherapeutic process, known as the Bonny Method of Guided Imagery and Music,[1] to induce imagery experiences through listening to excerpts of Western classical music. This individualized and transformational technique requires expertise

---

[1] H. L. Bonny, and L. M. Savary, *Music & Your Mind: Listening with a New Consciousness* (Barrytown, New York: Station Town Press, 1990).

Association for Music and Imagery, www.ami-bonnymethod.org

on the part of a facilitator who has completed advanced training through three levels of certification. Any experience of imagery can be extremely powerful, so we want to make sure that yours is a safe and positive one.

No matter what arises for you while you use your imagination, you may want to talk with someone about your journey with the music when you have finished. Alternatively, you may be the type of person who likes to write in a journal. Being able to express and communicate your experience in some form may contribute significantly to a deeper understanding of yourself. So think about how you would like to communicate your experience. See what your mind does with this music.

3. Find Music to Enhance Your Imagination

The music you choose to practice this technique may be classical or contemporary, but we suggest instrumental music. It may be a piece that you associate with pleasant events or one that is specifically composed to evoke restful images. Commercial recordings of sounds of nature, with or without music, also might appeal to you. See if any of the music you selected in your Music Listening Log meets these criteria. We also suggest listening to the guided instructions (tracks 12 and 14) and a version of "Clair de Lune" performed on a therapeutic harp (track 13) on our accompanying CD. You may want to experiment with different musical selections by closing your eyes while you let the music set some lovely scenes.

4. Start with a Relaxed Body

Use any of the music programs in chapter 5, "Body and Breath," to identify any tension in your body, and work it out with your breath, movement, massage, or progressive muscle relaxation. If you have been practicing regularly, it may not take long to relax your body.

5. Find Your Utopia

Close your eyes and let the music guide you to a place where you would like to be—a place you associate with positive feelings and tranquility. As the music goes on, explore this space in your mind's eye. Wander through this wonderful spot, taking time to appreciate its beauty and feel its warmth.

6. Discover a New Place

You may want to create a place where you have never been before. Use your imagination to design an imaginary utopia. You could be surprised at the scope of your creative potential.

7. Discover the Power of Music

This exercise may be a potent one. It may evoke ideas and feelings that not have surfaced before. As you express yourself to someone you trust or in your journal, communicate your unique experience. If, on the other hand, you have not been able to conjure up an image or memory, try it with another piece of music, or simply know that this technique may not meet your needs at this time. There are more music programs to come, and you may find other techniques more helpful for managing your stress and pain.

8. Draw the Experience

At the completion of this exercise, you may wish to explore your images in art. If you enjoy drawing or painting, color and form may express your mood better than words. You can write down features of your images or develop them by sculpting or representing them in another art form. Use your Music Plan Worksheet to assess the effects that "Sensing Peaceful Images" had on you. Then challenge your creativity by artistically representing your special place.

DISCOVERING YOUR IMAGINATION

TRACK 15

We understand that you may require more guidance to experience imagery while listening to music. Track 15 on our accompanying CD is "Discovering Your Imagination," a guided imagery exercise with Susan's spoken suggestions that guide you to a favorite place, while you listen to "Lullaby," composed and recorded by Daniel Kobialka. This program is another music-assisted relaxation and imagery (MARI) experience for you.

1. Let Your Mind Guide You

Sit or lie down in a quiet, safe place where your body is supported comfortably. Preparing a special space for yourself is an important part of this process. Remember to turn off electronic devices like cell phones or pagers, and ask other family members to avoid disturbing you during your imagery experience. For your own safety, do not play this recording while driving a vehicle or operating equipment.

What you imagine becomes real to your body: your body will tell you that you are in a relaxing place by releasing its tension. Your body will tighten up if you come to a place where you don't feel comfortable. Trust your mind to take you to the place where you will find what you need, and trust your body to let you know when you have arrived. Your imagination may be explored through any or all of your senses. Notice what you see, hear, taste, smell, and feel. If you become uncomfortable while listening, simply open your eyes and rest quietly for a few minutes.

2. Trust the Process

Your mind is capable of creating worlds near and far, realistic and fantastical. Guiding your imagination is a process. Allow it to unfold. You may see things more vividly as you begin to hear the music more fully. Let your mind travel and enjoy the adventure, or just take in the music. Take time to find music that elicits more images in your mind. If you practice this music program regularly during the next few weeks, you may find that you return to the same favorite location, or journey to a new, idyllic place that comforts you. Again, if you don't create images in your mind, that's not a problem. Take what the music brings for your mind, body, or spirit.

3. Let the Music Guide You

TRACK 16

Use the Music Plan Worksheet to note how effective "Discovering Your Imagination" has been for you. Just as in the previous music program, you may wish to use expressive writing or artwork to communicate your experience. These creative outlets offer opportunities to explore your imagination further. Once you have experienced the guided excursion through your mind on track 15, you may wish to listen to the music again. Track 16 includes Kobialka's "Lullaby" without any verbal guidance. We hope that you enjoy this music while you let it take you to a place in your mind that you wish or need to visit.

4. Try More Guided Imagery Experiences

There are many commercial recordings of nature sounds, and music to enhance your imagery. However, we particularly recommend finding a trained facilitator to take your listening experiences deeper and further.

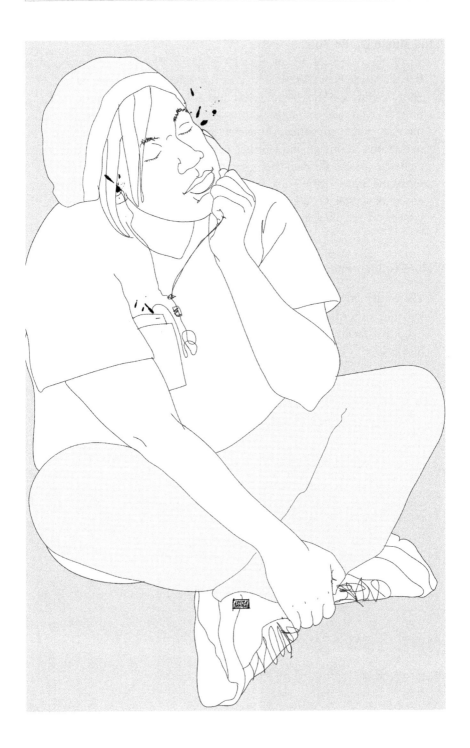

CHAPTER 7

Through Your Mind
to Your Body

My heart is bleeding
Memory-flooded music
Equilibrium

—Suzanne B. Hanser

FOCUS YOUR ATTENTION

Imagine that you had a tooth removed a few hours ago and your mouth is aching. It seems as though all you can think about is the hurt. You sit down in your easy chair, grab the remote control, and flip channels on the television set. You pause briefly on a program that catches your attention. Could it be? Ah, yes—it is a movie that you have not seen in at least twenty years. You hear the familiar theme song, and you are drawn into the action. Before you know it, two hours have passed, and you are barely aware of your toothache. Why? You focused your attention away from the pain.

Have you had such an experience? If so, you already know the possibility of diverting your mind from pain and distress. Music can offer you just such a distraction. In Susan's years of living with chronic pain, she has learned about the power of music to help herself to cope. "When I have an appointment for a procedure that I know will cause discomfort, I bring my portable music player with my favorite music. When I remember that music is able to help, I feel reassured that I will be all right."

1. Find Attention-Getting Music

Did you find selections in your Music Listening Log that meet the criteria for attention-focusing music? You may recall that we suggest identifying music with a driving rhythm or steady beat. The strength of the rhythm may move your body literally, and your tapping feet or snapping fingers may keep you attentive to your response to the music. Songs with lyrics that speak to you or elicit a strong, positive emotional response are also good candidates for this exercise. The most meaningful music that evokes memories and images will keep your mind occupied with these effects. The result may be that your attention is flooded with all those positive things that come with the music, rather than the distressing circumstances around you. Do you have some favorite songs from your teenage years or show tunes from a musical you love? Perhaps you prefer instrumental music that brings to mind a memorable occasion or milestone in your life. Try a selection with a strong, upbeat rhythm, varied dynamics, and musical changes that keep your interest throughout the piece. The energizing music in your playlist may provide just what you need to help you revisit a wonderful time in your life. While it engages your brain in remembering, imagining, changing your mood, moving your body, or paying attention to elements of the music, there's hardly room for the pain.

2. Immerse in the Music

The best time to begin listening to your music is before the pain or stress is acute. For example, start listening to your favorite upbeat music before an injection or a blood draw. You may be surprised to find that if you immerse yourself in the music, you may barely feel the needle. When the effect of a prescribed pain medication is diminishing, music may help you manage your pain before you are able to take your next dose. You may even find that you require less medication in combination with the music.

3. Experiment and Evaluate

Try an experiment. At a time of discomfort, use the scale located on the Pain Assessment or Stress Assessment Log to rate your pain or stress before you begin to listen to the music. Then rate yourself again after you have listened for at least thirty minutes. Do you notice any difference in your experience of the pain or stress? Experiment with different selections of music and different lengths of listening time until you discover what is most appropriate for you. You may use the Music Plan Worksheet to note how helpful "Focus Your Attention" has been for you.

Consider using this music the next time you expect to be distressed or in pain. Also plan to practice some of the most effective music programs along with the music that you have identified as attention-getting or energetic.

CREATIVE PROBLEM-SOLVING

After practicing the previous music programs, you may have already conditioned a positive sensory response to your music. If you found that pleasant images were able to replace worries and concerns while you listened, you are ready to try "Creative Problem-Solving." This program assumes that you have allowed yourself to relax your mind and successfully imagine a peaceful setting. It directs your images to suit your specific needs. Perhaps, you have been avoiding taking some action for fear of the consequences. You may have been putting off making a decision about something. Possibly, you have had difficulty motivating yourself to consider some future plans. Or you may be dealing with a stressful situation right now. Sometimes it is the expectation of the problem that is the worst part of dealing with it. When you are able to overcome worry or fear by enacting the dreaded activity in your mind and viewing potential solutions, you can feel more in control of the situation. In these instances, you can experience the events that cause you distress in the safety of your mind's eye, as you think of appropriate and successful ways to deal with this problem.

In many cases, the assistance of a music therapist or other professional is necessary to offer feedback and guidance in this process of problem solving. Therefore, as you begin to practice some of these techniques, avoid problems that are associated with strong emotions or long-term issues. We hope that you have already mastered some techniques to change your mood and to take you far away from your problems. "Creative problem-solving" introduces a method for handling your stressors head-on.

1. Identify the Stressor

Stressors come in many varieties. These are the things that make your life difficult. Many require some action to alter the troubled transaction. They may be in the form of:

- fearful situations—the upcoming appointment with your physician, the visit with relatives whom you have avoided in the past, or an important job interview or presentation

- trouble interacting with people—an argument with your loved one or difficulty communicating with your co-worker or boss

- lack of motivation—your inability to do something you have been putting off for a long time

- anxiety-laden events—discussing your financial situation with an auditor, or dealing with a litigation or legal problem

- lack of organization—having trouble being method-ical in your thinking or in structuring priorities

- difficulty making decisions—making the simplest daily lunch choice or more complex decisions with long-term consequences.

2. Recognize Your Pain

You may experience physical pain in parts of your body, or you may be dealing with mental or emotional pain. Admitting to yourself that you are in pain is a first step toward discovering ways to manage that pain. The experience of pain can be highly stressful and a stressful experience can increase your pain. This leads to a very vicious cycle that can spiral you down into great distress or depression before you know it.

Review both your Stress Assessment and Pain Assessment Logs to determine the problems that are causing you difficulty at this time. Identify one area to work on during this music program.

3. Begin Simply

Choose one situation that involves an upcoming stressful event. Start with a relatively simple problem over which you feel some control and confidence in its resolution. As you gain more experience and skill at this technique, you may want to tackle more resistant stressors, including pain.

4. Use Music that has Guided You to Peaceful Settings

The music that has been most successful in eliciting positive imagery offers the most suitable beginning for this problem-solving session. If you have not experienced imagery with music, then play something that evokes a soothing mood or sense of comfort.

5. Start with a Relaxed Body

Use one of the music programs in chapter 5, "Body and Breath," to relax your body. Remember to breathe deeply and rhythmically.

6. Go to a Relaxing Place

Close your eyes, and let the music guide you to a place where you would like to be. As the music continues, explore this place. Take as much time as you deem necessary to create an appropriate setting.

7. Create a Place to Problem-Solve

Slowly introduce a new setting—the one in which you face the problem you are about to confront. Focus your thoughts on a way to approach this problem. For a fearful situation, place yourself in that environment and see yourself moving forward to approach the feared condition, while you remain in this relaxed state. If your problem involves interpersonal relationships, try out some ways of communicating, and observe the response in your imagination. For events that you have been avoiding, take action in your mind's eye. If organization or decision making is stressful, picture yourself actually making some changes while you still maintain a relaxed body. When dealing with a painful situation, imagine yourself accepting the pain, and release some aspect of the pain as you attend to the familiar and reassuring tone of the music.

8. Start the Process

What is the very first step you will take in your plan to deal with the problem? Check to ensure that you are feeling relaxed. Then imagine yourself carrying out this important step, whether it is facing your fear, engaging in a difficult conversation, performing an aversive activity, or the like. Still feeling relaxed? Then rehearse another step in your plan. If you begin to feel tense or anxious, return to your relaxing place, and regain your calm and pleasant emotions. Wait for another session to introduce the problem again.

If you are able to visualize these scenarios without distress, continue to see yourself taking each step in the process of acting out a possible way to cope with your problem. When you develop confidence in your ability to deal with this issue, you are ready to try out your plan for real.

9. Find a Creative Solution

Carry out this exercise as long as it is comfortable. Attempt alternate routes to solutions. Most important, relax and enjoy the music while you explore creative ways to cope with your problems and deal with the stress and pain in your life.

10. Evaluate

Use the Music Plan Worksheet to note how effective "Creative Problem Solving" has been for you. If you had a successful experience, try it with another challenge that has been eluding you. Also engage in some of the most effective music programs along with music listening to enhance the impact. Then reevaluate by taking some notes to remind you of your progress. Emphasize any changes in your identified perspective, recognizing that these first attempts are significant in overcoming your difficulty.

LULLABY AND GOOD NIGHT

TRACK 15, 16

"Lullaby and Good Night" helps you enhance a good night's sleep. Whether you have difficulty falling asleep or find yourself awakening in the middle of the night, listening to music may assist you to relax and float off to sleep. Once you have learned to relax with music, you may select your favorite stress-reducing music and the music program that has achieved the greatest success for you. There are also certain guidelines to take into account as you maximize your chances for a restful sleep.

Follow These Simple Guidelines

- Avoid taking a nap during the day.

- Avoid caffeine and exercise at least four hours before going to bed.

- Go to sleep at the same hour each night, and plan to awaken at the same time each morning.

- Use your bed for sleeping, but not snacking, television watching, or other activities that might interfere with a good night's sleep. You want to associate going to bed with going to sleep.

- Wait until you feel tired to go to bed.

- If you awaken and are unable to get back to sleep with music, leave the bedroom and do something else until you feel very tired. Likewise, if you are listening to music in the middle of the night, and worries or negative thoughts take over, leave the bed.

1. Listen to Music that You Find Relaxing

Two types of music bring the highest probability of success in aiding relaxation: music with calming and comforting associations and music that is repetitious or monotonous. The music that conjures up tranquil images may be very advantageous in helping you get to sleep. However, some people give so much attention to the process of listening that it actually interferes with falling asleep. In this case, repetitious sounds, such as recorded ocean waves or ambient music (with limited new musical material or variations in tempo, dynamics, or tonality) may be preferable.

2. Use Familiar Music

Most importantly, listen to music that is familiar and predictable, offering no surprises. This is not the time to try out a new recording. Once you have identified music that is restful to you, listen to the same music each night at bedtime. Over time, your body and mind will associate that particular music with falling asleep. Review your Music Listening Log to determine the most calming music you know. Did you select some music for your sleep-inducing playlist? If not, try Kobialka's "Lullaby" on track 16.

3. Start with a Relaxed Body and Mind

Use any of the preceding music programs to relax your body and mind. Breathe deeply, and let the music relax you totally.

4. Remember Your Relaxation Lessons

Close your eyes, and let the music guide you to an even deeper state of rest and sleep. Just as in previous exercises, try to maintain a pleasant and relaxed state while listening to music. Should something interfere with this relaxation, turn off the music or leave the bed. When you begin to feel tired, return to your bed, and practice your most successful techniques.

5. Enjoy a Restful Sleep

Use the Music Plan Worksheet to note how effective "Lullaby and Good Night" has been for you. You have mastered the relaxation skills necessary to maximize your chances of a restful night's sleep. The music is a gentle reminder to sleep and dream peacefully.

A MUSICAL BOOST

Music is versatile. As you know, music evokes many moods. Not only can it relax you, but it can stimulate as well. "A Musical Boost" provides a way to amplify your energy and invigorate you.

Perhaps you have difficulty getting going in the morning. Is there a low point in your day when you tend to become tired or depressed? Do you have problems motivating yourself to take action on an issue of concern? This program uses music to enhance your energy while lifting your mood.

1. Use Energy-Boosting Music

You have become adept at identifying music to evoke the right mood. You have learned to listen for the elements that make a certain piece of music relaxing. Now you can find the music that will help revitalize you.

First try some of your favorite music that you included in your energizing music playlist. If you didn't add any music to this category, think about music that is associated with an uplifting feeling. Try to find music that has a solid beat and is in a major key. Most important, identify music that makes you feel upbeat and makes you want to move.

Many people find that fast and exciting music is so very different from their present mood that it fails to elicit change. For this reason, it is advisable to match your mood with a musical selection, and gradually change the music. We music therapists call this the *iso-principle*—iso means same.[1] You might start with your relaxing music playlist or some slow music with long, flowing phrases. The next selection could be faster and more expressive. The next piece might have a stronger rhythm and louder accents. Well-chosen music will bring up positive associations and a livelier mood as it continues. Try some of the music that is in your spiritual music playlist. This uplifting music may also bring you into a new state of mind.

2. Let Your Music Set the Mood

Enjoy the music. Enjoy the mood. Approach your day with this beautiful music in mind. Prepare yourself for the rest of the day. Move to the music as you gradually feel energy filling your body. Be as active as you feel comfortable. Start small, moving your fingers and toes. Then, stretch your arms and legs. Open your mouth wide. Reach out and welcome whatever your day might bring. Open yourself to a new day!

Give yourself time to get into the mood of the music. If your movements are too fast, you could begin to feel agitated. Make sure that your body feels free of tension and that you are able to feel yourself moving freely and easily. Turn your actions into a dance. Then, wind down with a relaxation strategy of your choice.

[1] E. L. Gatewood, "The Psychology of Music in Relation to Anesthesia," *American Journal of Surgery Anesthesia Supplement* 35 (1921): 47–50; L. Montello, *Essential Musical Intelligence*, Wheaton, IL: Quest Books, 2002.

3. Think Music

Your body is relaxed and feeling good. Review your Stress Assessment Log. Look at those negative thoughts that plague you throughout the day. Replace your destructive thoughts with positive, constructive thinking that refutes them. Substitute "I will" for any "I can't" on your list. Turn around the "nos" and "nots" with the "yesses" associated with possibility and hope. Repeat "A Musical Boost," and find more encouraging vocabulary for the self-talk that tells you how to feel. Use the Music Plan Worksheet to note how effective "A Musical Boost" has been for you.

Now it's time to turn your thoughts to what awaits you during the day. What are the positive aspects of your day ahead? What are you looking forward to today? How can you make your day more pleasant? Bring your music along, and put it on when you need some pepping up. Think positive thoughts, and think music!

CHAPTER 8

Singing and Chanting

"To Sing as One"

To sing music with the choir
Is to live and breathe
A unified feeling,
Fulfilling to perceive.

Inhale, center, and prepare.
Release blended tone.
Voices merge together,
Weave the strands of sound.

Each singer's privileged to express
Uniquely from the soul,
While sensitive to others
To convey harmonious whole.

Individual tones distinctly
Resonate a section,
Whose meaning's heard in context
Of the composition.

Significance of the choir
Echoes in humanity.
We reverberate as one
With collective energy.

My personal expression
Impacts the lives of others.
May I convey empathically,
Connected—as one together.

—Susan E. Mandel

SINGING

Do you ever sing in the shower? Do you hum along with the radio? Are you an aspiring rock star, but were told not to quit your day job? It's true that few of us will become singing superstars, but all of us have the ability to express our unique selves through our voices. Your voice is your natural instrument. It is all yours and like no one else's on the planet. You carry it with you wherever you go. Here is your chance to sing your heart out, even if you never thought of yourself as a singer.

You know that it is healthy to allow yourself to express your emotions. So here's a prescription to sing them out. Preliminary research shows that singing enhances immune function,[1] so sing on and sing often to stay hale and hearty!

1. Tune In

Take a deep breath in through your nose to your belly, and let it out slowly through your mouth, as you sustain a long tone on "aaah." Feel your body vibrate in resonance with the note. With the next breath, exhale a sigh. To do this, start with a high note and slide down to the lowest note you can reach, all in one breath. Now reverse direction, starting with the lowest pitch, and letting it rise gradually higher and higher. In order to sing, you automatically breathe and release tension. You're exercising your vocal range and massaging your insides in the process.

2. Sing Your Favorite Song

You're ready to exercise your voice with a piece that you love. You can play your favorite song and sing along, or if you know a song well, all you need to do is sing. Really sing it out. Pay attention to the lyrics and express the feelings behind the words. Sing it to yourself, or sing it to someone who appreciates your voice.

3. Cherish Your Voice

Perhaps you think you can't sing. That may be because someone has told you that you can't hold a tune or that your voice doesn't sound pleasing. Too many people we know have been asked to mouth the

[1] G. Kreutz et al., "Effects of Choir Singing or Listening on Secretory Immunoglobulin A, Cortisol, and Emotional State," *Journal of Behavioral Medicine* 27, no. 6 (2004): 623–635.

words when they sang in a choir. By the way, some of those people are the ones who get the most pleasure out of singing! Do you ever say, "I can't sing," or do you only allow yourself to sing in the shower? Actually, you can sing anywhere, and unless you're planning to sell your recordings, getting pleasure out of singing doesn't have anything to do with talent or innate ability.

4. Evaluate

Use the Music Plan Worksheet to note the impact of your singing. If you enjoy singing, do it more. Can you commit to using your voice more today than you did yesterday? That's a promise you can make to yourself. Stick with it, and see if there is extra joy in your day.

5. Sing with Others

Consider joining a chorus, where you participate with others who value singing. Who knows? You might even make some new friends. Singing with a group allows you to share music and energy. Each person's voice contributes to the blended sound, and you can feel the unity of a special community who love to express themselves in this way.

6. Improve Your Voice

Professional singers are not born with the voices you hear from the stage. They have been trained to make the most of their talent. They have practiced scales and exercises for countless hours to prepare for their solos. They have sung songs over and over, to memorize every note and word, and to work on musical interpretation. You know the adage, "Practice makes perfect," and nowhere is practice more important than in singing or playing an instrument. Developing your natural instrument, your voice, is a skill you carry with you everywhere.

Consider taking a voice lesson to get the most out of your voice. Sometimes, embracing a challenge, like learning a new song or enhancing the quality of your voice, can prove to be a fulfilling journey that offers you a sense of accomplishment and well-being. Improving your vocal technique or increasing your repertoire can help you to focus on your capabilities while you enjoy yourself.

7. Heed a Caveat

Be reasonable with yourself. If you set an unrealistic goal that is beyond what is possible for you to achieve, given your vocal ability or range, you may experience more stress than fulfillment. The key is to enjoy the journey and take a moment to appreciate learning a new song or making new strides in the use of your voice. When you are self-critical, adjust your expectations so that you can be successful. Value the abilities that you have, like being able to remember the lyrics of a favorite song, or reaching a high note. Recognize and take pride in your improvement. If you observe your positive and negative reactions to the singing experience, you may learn a great deal about how you treat yourself in general. When you constantly find fault with yourself, or think derogatory things about your singing abilities, you are holding yourself back from appreciating the progress that you are making. It is too easy to be your own worst enemy. Make an effort to be kind to yourself and show yourself the patience that you would show a friend. Be particularly aware of your expectations. Set small, realistic goals for your progress. Be proud when you reach your goals, and take credit when you exceed them. Learning to sing is like unpeeling an onion; you work through one layer to reveal the next and then the one that follows. Enjoy each layer of self-discovery. You will experience an endless opportunity to learn and to grow.

8. Experience Flow

Mihaly Csikszentmihaly[2] has researched the idea of *flow*, a sense of being totally immersed in an activity such that you feel energized and ultimately successful. You can experience being "in the flow" with your voice when you sing something you never thought would ever sound so good. To maximize the opportunities to experience this truly high feeling, choose songs that remain within your vocal range and ability. Find the right balance of challenge and success in your choices, and you too may enjoy this peak experience.

[2] M. Csikszentmihaly, *Flow: The Psychology of Optimal Experience* (New York: Harper & Row, 1990).

CHANTING

Chant is an ancient form of spiritual practice that is observed in almost every religion. Chanting is a most simplistic form of song, as it uses one or a few notes, repeated over and over. It may be sung or spoken rhythmically, and is ritually based on the name of God or a significant prayer or text. In many traditions, sacred chanting is a way of communicating with the divine. It is said to release a healing form of energy and flow that welcomes a spiritual presence.

Contemporary chants are prevalent in secular settings, from protest marches to sports events, where they incite and unify people in a common cause, or excite home team fans. While religious mantras and psalms are meant to invite introspection, these other chants are capable of provoking strong emotions and group behavior, as evidenced by the clashes amongst enthusiasts at many a tournament. Think of the power of a stadium filled with people who are chanting the name of their favorite athlete in loud unison.

Gregorian chants were the first songs that led to what we now know as Western music. Today we come full circle to rap music, a form that is more chant than song, and a genre that has taken off as part of worldwide hip-hop culture. Although introspective, spiritual chant is customarily practiced within a religious community. It is possible to benefit from chanting to instill either a sense of calm or a source of motivation. It takes only a few minutes to give yourself the gifts of chant, but that may be all that is required to allow you a respite from a stressful time, an opportunity to prepare for the rest of your day, or a moment to take stock of where you are, and rejuvenate. As with other intense experiences that may be provoked by suggestions in this book, we advise you to find an outlet for thoughts and emotions that may surface during your chanting practice. You may choose to write in a journal, to reach out to a compassionate friend, or to communicate with your spiritual or religious advisor about your experiences.

1. Identify a Meaningful Word or Phrase

Is there some name or word that is important to you? Do the words "peace," "love," or "calm" resonate with you? Find an affirmation or favorite line of poetry, or make one up, like "I feel peace," "I can be who I want to be," or "I can do it." You can also create a sound or syllable that is soothing to you. For example, the sound "ah" is common to the divine name in many cultures. Or you may choose to chant a line from your favorite prayer.

2. Go Inward

When you find just the right words or sounds, close your eyes. Say or sing them, slowly and calmly. Find the rhythm and pace that suits you, and continue to repeat your special chant. You may find that your voice gravitates to a particular tone or pitch, or that your voice moves freely in its own pattern. Allow yourself to experience what evolves within you. When it seems right to stop, notice what happens in the silence. Pay attention to your feelings and thoughts, acknowledge them, and appreciate them.

3. Find Your Inner Motivation

You can also create a chant to give yourself an inner pep talk—a self-affirmation. Think about what you need right now. Is it acceptance? Is it meaning? You have all the resources within you that are required; you only need to access them. Find the sound, word, or phrase that represents a helpful, positive thought. It may be as simple as "I am me," or as profound as "There is a reason that I am here on earth." As you repeat your unique chant, let it fill you with exactly what you need.

4. Evaluate

Use the Music Plan Worksheet to note how you react to "Chanting."

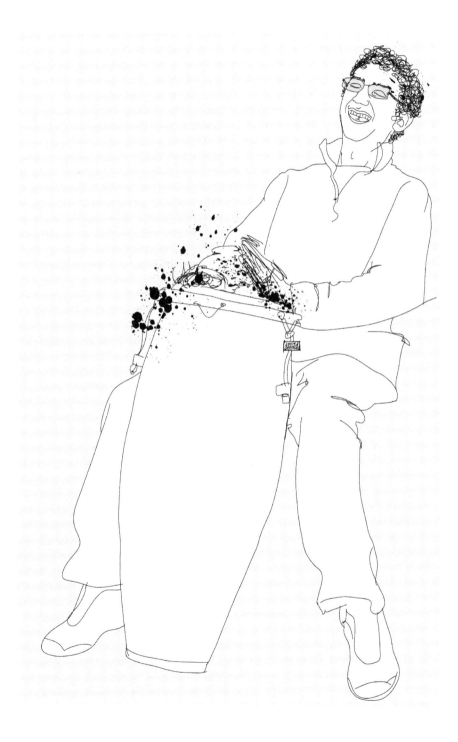

CHAPTER 9

Songwriting

Write a song today
Your soul has something to say
Let it sing away

—Suzanne B. Hanser

You might be thinking, "Well, I could never write a song." But there are several reasons why you might wish to try. First, original songs offer an expressive outlet for your feelings, enabling you to gain insight and awareness surrounding your personal challenges. Secondly, your songs can give voice to your own problem-solving strategies. For example, your song can include affirmations that remind you of positive ways of thinking or approaching your difficulties, whenever you sing or hear it. A third reason for songwriting is that if you decide to write a song for another person, you are giving the greatest gift: a creation from your heart. This act also takes the focus off your issues and may contribute to your sense of altruism and generosity. The fourth reason is that it can be easier than you think to write a song.

In her work at Dana-Farber Cancer Institute, Suzanne has encouraged many people to compose songs as a way to express something they wish to say to a loved one, communicate their own experiences to others, or simply take part in an original, creative process. Individuals have created songs about what it is like to have cancer, songs for unborn grandchildren, and songs that affirm life. Some hummed new melodies, some put favorite sayings to favorite tunes, and others spontaneously beat the rhythm of their words on drums. Somehow, with a little help, everyone who had the desire managed to write music that carried special meaning.

According to a recent *New York Times* interview, 24-year-old Melody Gardot didn't know that she was meant to write songs. It wasn't until a near fatal accident and her referral to music therapy six years ago that she discovered she had a talent for songwriting. She learned to play guitar while in a body cast, and wrote songs of her pain and recovery. Her first CD, *Worrisome Heart*, is filled with life's lessons; her second, *My One and Only Thrill*, sold over half a million albums in Europe. After her accident, she explained, "Sometimes you have to be broken down to your core to get back to your essence."[1] She has certainly found that beauty resides inside her broken body and can be shared through her heartfelt songs.

We don't know if you have latent talent for songwriting, but you will never know what you can create if you don't give it a try. As you experiment with "Songwriting," use the Music Plan Worksheet to note what our songwriting methods did for you.

WRITE SOME LYRICS

It doesn't matter whether you start with lyrics or music. Perhaps the easiest way to write a song is to substitute some words here and there to personalize a tune that you like. It is simple to substitute your name or someone you care about for "Maria" in the *West Side Story* aria, or for "Peggy Sue" in the Buddy Holly melody. You can also take out the words that end a phrase and substitute your own. For example, what do you want to lay down by the riverside? In Susan's work with people enrolled in cardiac rehabilitation, one commuter sang, "I'm going to lay down rush-hour traffic down by the riverside," while a hassled police officer added, "I'm going to lay down emergencies...." You can try filling in a few words of your own while singing along with a familiar melody you hear on the radio or a commercial jingle that interrupts your favorite television program.

1. Find Meaningful Words

There are many ways to find lyrics that carry a message you want to communicate. Do you have a favorite poem or book of poetry? Is there some prose or an affirmation that is important to you? Is there a letter you have written or received? If you keep a journal, is there a memorable page? If nothing special comes to mind, ask a friend, family member, or acquaintance to write some words to you, or suggest their favorite sayings.

---

[1] S. Holden, "From Death's Door to Earning the Keys to the World," *New York Times* (October 14, 2009), http://www.nytimes.com/2009/10/15/arts/music/15gardot.html

You can also write something yourself. Write about someone you know: a pet, a place, or a hobby that you enjoy. Write about something that affirms who you are. Your lyrics don't have to be lengthy because you can repeat them over and over with different musical accompaniments. They don't have to rhyme, so unless rhyming comes naturally to you, don't worry about how the lines fit together. Sometimes, the shortest phrase is able to capture the essence of what you want to say.

Creating song lyrics can be a fun—or very serious—way to express yourself. Susan enjoys writing parodies of familiar songs for special occasions. For a recent wedding shower, she asked the bride questions about her favorites and substituted lyrics to "My Favorite Things."

Pizza and pasta, pot stickers and grilled cheese,
Almond bread, brownies, and chocolate-chip cookies,
Tennis and softball, and Indians too.
Jennifer's favorites? These are a few.

Purple and turquoise, sunflowers, and daisies,
Gatsby, The Hobbit, *Meir, and DaVinci,*
Wizard of Oz, Bewitched, *and* The West Wing
These are a few of her favorite things.

Meant for each other, they first met at Princeton.
He likes the Yankees—oh well, she still loves him.
Years back and forth, they're together at last.
He popped the question, her answer was yes.

Adam and JJ,
Next year in May
Bride and groom you'll be.
We love you and wish you a lifetime of love
To share all your favorite things.

2. Express How You Feel

Free associate and see what comes out. Take a pen and just start writing. Give yourself a prompt, like "I am …" or "I like …" or decide on a subject for your free writing. Once it starts to flow, let it all out. Keep on writing until you have said all you want to say.

3. Write Yourself an Affirmation

After you have communicated your feelings, turn your attention to some statements that inspire you to move beyond your stress and pain. Focus on your abilities and strengths. Consider the following lines of optimism:

> *I can do it.*

> *Right now all is well.*

> *I'm shaky, but I can cope.*

> *I'm doing my best.*

> *Although today is tough, I expect tomorrow to be better.*

Empty optimism won't work in this exercise. It is better that the lyrics speak to you and your experience. Go back to your Stress Assessment Log. If you found that the stress in your life resulted in negative thinking, you have some ready-made lyrics. Use those very words, and add some phrases that dispute your thoughts. Here's an example from a born worrier:

Negative thoughts: "I can't stop worrying. I'll never change. Life will always be difficult for me."

Challenge those thoughts with: "I can choose to stop worrying. Even I can change if I put my mind to it. Life has been really hard, but tomorrow could be better."

Compose lyrics for the chorus: "I can choose to stop worrying. I can change. Life can be better tomorrow."

Say the words and see how they flow. Add or take away a few words to make the rhythm of the lines feel right. Exaggerate the phrases so that they sound a little more musical. Try them with a simple melody. Our worrier edited the words, and set them to "I've Been Working on the Railroad."

I can't stop myself from worrying.
And I'll never change.
I can't stop myself from worrying.
I've been doing it for ages.
Life has really been quite awful,
difficult and tough,
Life has always been a struggle,
troublesome and rough.
Chorus:
Even I can change
Even I can change
I can try a day without worrying.
Even I can change
Even I can change
Tomorrow I'll go worry-free.
I can put my mind to it.
Put all my worries behind me.
If I can put my mind to it,
Tomorrow'll be a better day for me.

This songwriter finds herself singing this ditty to herself when she begins to worry. It refocuses her thinking and arrests the spiral of negative thoughts. You, too, can try your hand at putting your honest and affirmative words to work in a familiar song. When you are ready, play a recording of a song that is simple to sing. Then find a way to edit your words to fit the musical phrases.

Write about the things that give you joy. Write about the things for which you are grateful. Write about your hopes and dreams. A little humor goes a long way, too. Funny words and silly songs put your problems into perspective. When you can laugh about those things that have caused the most consternation, you know that you are getting better at coping with them.

WRITE SOME MUSIC

Hum some short melodies into a portable recording device. Play them back and see which tunes set the mood you want or are catchy and melodious. Keep track of the most hummable and memorable melodies. If you play a musical instrument, you have an advantage. You can play around and find something to fit your mood. If you don't have formal music training, ask someone to notate your melodies so they can be preserved. Record everything you do so that you can sort out what you will use for your songs later. Some people find that the music inspires words and thoughts. Have that recorder handy so that you can capture your spontaneous musical offerings. You may be surprised at what you can create!

Let the Computer Do the Work

There are a number of software programs that help you compose. JamStudio[2] shows you how to write a melody. The computer plays it back for you in your choice of instruments and styles. If you're young at heart, you'll enjoy the Tony-b machine.[3] This playful software provides you with a cartoon-like keyboard while it accompanies you with all sorts of dance rhythms. CreatingMusic.com[4] gives you a virtual pencil to write your notes and to select the instruments that play your music. Noteflight[5] is a more sophisticated program for notating your original music. It plays your piece, prints it, edits it, and if you're ready to share your creations online, publishes it for all to see. This is just a sampling of what is available online. By the time this book is published, there will be even more software available in the market. So if you've never tried making computer music, play around and challenge your creativity.

[2] www.jamstudio.com/Studio/index.htm

[3] www.tony-b.org

[4] www.creatingmusic.com

[5] www.noteflight.com/login

FROM YOUR MIND TO YOUR HEART

It is said that "music is the soul's own speech." Are there any lyrics from songs that come to your mind from your heart? If so, sing them out loud or write them down, whatever comes easiest to you. Experiment. Be playful, be serious, be whatever you want. Focus on the creative experience rather than the result. The impact of your songwriting may surprise you. That is exactly what happened to Susan's mother-in-law. After suffering traumatic injuries and the death of her husband in an automobile accident, Millie fully recovered, later welcomed the birth of her great grandchildren, and currently enjoys an excellent quality of life. Twenty years after her accident, she needs help boosting her spirit every morning. Millie wrote a song that she sings to herself in the shower. The words and melody that came to her bring her comfort daily.

> *Mildred Rose, Mildred Rose,*
> *Thank God.*
> *God is with you*
> *Allow God to come into your heart.*
> *God is with you.*
> *You have so much to be thankful for.*

WRITE FOR SOMEONE ELSE

If you have a way to record your song, you can give it away. If you don't, you can offer a private performance. What greater gift than something as personal as a piece of music composed just for someone you care about? Writing a song that communicates why you care about this person can help you focus on the people who support you. It can honor who they are or what they have done for you. Writing for or about someone else is a way to preserve and remind you about the gratitude that you feel.

CHAPTER 10

Playing an Instrument and Improvising

Sounds across the pond
Float into my heavy heart
Why am I lighter?

—Suzanne B. Hanser

PLAY ON

As a pianist, Suzanne has performed for many people, be they family, friends, colleagues, clients, or general audiences. No matter the venue, invariably someone will comment, "If only I could play like that." Suzanne remarks:

Taking the compliment graciously, I am thinking, "If only you knew what it took to play like this." I dare not count up the number of lessons I've taken over the decades, and the hours of practice required to meet my teachers' standards. When I consider what has kept me playing piano all these years, I know that the work and discipline have been rewarded many times over by my sense of mastery at being able to recreate a beautiful piece of music at the piano.

I have also had the pleasure of teaching adults who had always wanted to learn an instrument. At a young age, I was fortunate that my parents heeded my call for a piano, and was privileged to take lessons from teachers who uncovered my talent and encouraged me on.

It is never too late to discover the musical abilities that have lain dormant because you did not have these opportunities. We are not denying that some of us have more dexterity and can better coordinate our finger movements from one key to the next. Some of us can translate the written notes more easily than others. It is more natural for some to interpret the composer's notes and sew them together into a seamless melody. But we firmly believe that you who have never played an instrument have never tested your hidden talent. If you are motivated to meet your full creative potential, learning to play an instrument, or rediscovering an instrument you have played before, can offer a sense of accomplishment that is capable of feeding your self-esteem.

If you know something about a musical instrument you studied sometime in the past, rekindling a relationship with that instrument may be like reconnecting with an old friend. If, on the other hand, you have negative associations with learning or performing based on your past, know that your approach to music in adulthood will probably be quite different. With your current maturity and experience, your new teacher, and a fresh motivation for learning to play, your musical learning experience will be assuredly brighter.

TAKE A RISK

Are you ready to take on this challenge? It's risky to launch into something new or take another go at something that did not reap much pleasure some time ago. Making the commitment to learn and practice can be difficult and demanding, and you are not looking for another source of stress! Then, again, if you're game, the discipline that is required and a hearty dose of effort may lead the way to fulfillment. We must offer this caution: Playing an instrument may also transform your self-image into a successful, creative person.

1. Find a Musical Instrument You Love

We do believe that you are capable of producing beautiful music. You must find an instrument that is well suited to your physical ability and personal interests. Today, electronic keyboards can produce a rhythm section and set of chordal harmonies in a style of your choice. All you have to do to perform many well-known pieces is pick out their simple tunes. Software programs like GarageBand[1] allow you to write and record your music with a touch of your mouse, and more music programs are available every day. You can purchase electronic instruments and computer software that enable you to perform with less effort and practice than starting from scratch on an acoustic instrument that carries no amplification or electronics. If the piano appeals to you, you can take an interactive lesson on The Piano Page.[2] If contemporary music is more your thing, check out GuitarHero[3] and RockBand,[4] two programs that let you rock out in virtual reality. If you prefer to perform music instantly, you can purchase Wii games.[5] The BBC's Making Tracks[6] provides you with a bunch of musical games to learn and enjoy. With a portable MIDI keyboard and Mixcraft 4,[7] you can create all sorts of sounds.

We also suggest visiting your local music store, and trying your hand (and mouth in the case of the winds or brass) at a variety of real instruments. It may be difficult to produce a decent sound on many of these, particularly the strings, woodwinds, or brass, but notice your gut reaction to seeing these instruments. Also listen to some music you would love to play, and observe what instruments appeal to you.

2. Learn Your Lessons

Many music stores will rent instruments on a trial basis, and they may offer lessons, as well. If you decide to learn a new musical instrument, be sure you are ready to be patient with yourself, and able to focus on the small improvements you make. If you tend to be highly self-critical, learning an instrument could be an exercise in frustration. To optimize success, consider using your music lessons as a tutorial in how to be kind to yourself, and how to show yourself the consideration you would give your best friends. Determine the amount of time you can devote to lessons and practice, and plan your week accordingly. You might also seek out a teacher who has worked with adults, and with whom you sense a good rapport. Let prospective teachers know your goals,

[1] www.garageband.com

[2] www.netrover.com/~kingskid/piano/piano.html

[3] www.hub.guitarhero.com

[4] www.rockband.com

[5] www.wiimusic.com

[6] www.bbc.co.uk/orchestras/play

[7] www.acoustica.com/mixcraft

and ask them what musical accomplishments might be realistic for you. We understand that there are some advantages to learning to play an instrument during childhood, but your maturity, self-discipline, and perspective as an adult provide the ingredients for a meaningful learning experience.

Susan wanted to learn to play guitar since she sang at campfires during her childhood. She recalls:

> But it wasn't until completing my graduate studies that I decided to take guitar lessons. I could not have known the joy that awaited me when I showed up at my first lesson with Judy, a very talented local musician. As my skill increased with regular practice, I enjoyed playing the guitar to accompany sing-alongs with my children, their friends, and their classmates. Years later, they all fondly recall those shared musical moments. One sunny Fourth of July weekend, my world changed. My mother called to inform me that my father was hospitalized with a malignant brain tumor. Six months later, he died.
>
> Music sustained me throughout those months of my father's illness. I continued my guitar lessons and practiced for hours at a time, alone on my patio. (The neighbors were kind enough never to complain.) The lessons with Judy became support sessions, as we shared feelings about music and about our parents. After my dad died, I wrote a note to Judy, thanking her for being my "musical therapist." It was that experience with music that opened the door for me to study music therapy. As they say, "the rest is history!"

3. Evaluate

Use the Music Plan Worksheet to note your thoughts about learning to play an instrument. With a good teacher, regular practice, and recognition of every bit of progress along the way, you might find that you are feeling more fulfilled and that your stress level is diminishing every day. And who knows where the music may lead you?

IMPROVISE

Some of us get through life by improvising. Suzanne doesn't.

> *I want everything planned and perfect, and I don't like the unexpected. Fortunately, musical improvisation has taught me to lighten up, and stop taking myself so seriously. After a long history of performing every note with a seriousness of purpose and the exactitude of a perfectionist, I have begun to improvise on instruments I encounter or create, and lately, on piano.*

> *So, I took a risk. I played a drum along with one of my favorite pieces, Ravel's* Bolero. *This orchestral piece gets louder and louder, and while I accompanied the intensifying rhythm, I felt my heartbeat quicken. The music became thicker and stronger as it continued, and while I beat away, I let myself go and pounded my heart out. My energy rose with the music, and somehow, I was able to release the tension I had been feeling. I didn't have to scream or throw something. I let my energy explode like a cymbal crash.*

On a sunny afternoon, when your authors took a break from writing this book, we emerged from behind our computers and went outside. Susan heard the inviting sound of the Native American flute in the distance, and found Suzanne facing the trees and playing. Susan brought out her Native American drum and began drumming along.

> *We played in harmony, our synchronized improvisation a symbol of our relationship, and just the inspiration we needed to return to our collective writing.*

1. Keep the Beat

You, too, can play a drum—or a pot or a table, if you don't happen to have a drum around. Keeping the beat can be grounding. For one thing, the rhythm is predictable when you feel like there are too many things you can't foresee. For another, keeping the beat structures your movement and energy in a way that is natural. We are rhythmic beings whose heart and circulation adhere to our body's life-affirming tempo. When our limbs are in order, we walk or run in strict rhythm, and that helps keep us balanced. Furthermore, when we beat along with music, we become part of the process of creating that music. How empowering is that?

2. Try a New Way

I have to admit, when I can't figure out what to do, I have to improvise. I do it in the kitchen when the ingredients for a recipe can't be found. I end up with some very unusual substitutions, but invariably, the dish comes out better than ever before. Similarly, when I'm in my garden, and don't have the proper implements for planting, I improvise and nature provides some tools, like rocks and leaves. The job gets done, but in the process, I discover some beautiful stones for ornamentation.

—Suzanne B. Hanser

Improvising is what we do without preparation or instruction. We do what feels right or comes naturally, while we try out something that we might never have thought of doing, otherwise. What happens is not predictable, but it often leads to a surprisingly successful outcome. The spontaneity of improvisation is radically different from the goal-directed activity that tends to rule the workday, if not the whole day, of busy people. Trying something new can redirect your perspective and give you a new way of approaching old problems.

So it is for musical improvisation. When Suzanne is not reading music or playing a song that she knows, she can fool around at the piano, trying out some new combinations of notes or chords. "Sometimes it sounds really awful, and sometimes I can't believe that I found notes that work so well together. I also have a secret. I like playing the black keys of the piano." These notes comprise a pentatonic scale—a common scale throughout the world, and any combination of its notes sound pretty good. It is easy to play around and generate novel effects using just these notes. "The result is astonishment that I can compose such lovely music." Try it next time you are around a piano or keyboard.

3. Make Something Up

Sometimes Suzanne makes up melodies, singing them on "doodly-do," and listening for what comes out. She observes:

> *Of course, that's often when I am in the car or alone. But, for me, improvising takes some of the pressure off having to sing or play the "right" note. It brings out my creativity and playfulness. I feel like a child who is running around without a care, unconcerned about what others think of the sounds I am creating. I am really myself—my song is uniquely mine, and it has never been heard before.*

Would you like to feel younger? Try composing a song, find the silliest lyrics, and sing out strong.

Susan experienced that sense of playfulness when she composed humorous lyrics about her teenage daughter. "I spontaneously combined many of my daughter's nicknames as a substitute for the lyrics of 'Supercalifragilisticexpialidocious' from *Mary Poppins.*

> *Precious pumpernickel pudding pie dear darling daughter*
> *Even though she doesn't listen every time she ought-er*
> *And says "I need it" even when*
> *It's something we just bought her*
> *Precious pumpernickel pudding pie dear darling daughter*

Susan remarked, "I had fun creating and singing this song, but I need to share a word of caution: Singing it to my daughter's girlfriends at her sixteenth birthday party may not have been advisable!"

4. Join Together

Improvisation often occurs in groups or ensembles. Jazz is a musical genre based on each player's ability to improvise. Some professional musicians devote their careers to mastering the art of improvisation, so while the music may sound spontaneous, it may be highly evolved from techniques that the musicians have studied and performed for a long time. As they play together repeatedly, they learn to read one another. You, too, might study with a jazz musician or a gifted teacher of improvisation.

Drum circles are another means of group improvisation that are popping up the world over. Drumming is an ancient spiritual practice that has been adapted as a recreational activity to bring people together. Many people find great social support in the unifying beat, and often feel that a repetitive and grounding beat is mesmerizing and relaxing. Dr. Barry Bittman and colleagues have researched the impact of group drumming and found evidence to support its ability to counteract the stress response.[8] Local drum circles have become a popular way for people to get together and express themselves. You can search the Internet for drum circles in your neighborhood.

5. Consult a Music Therapist

Music therapists use a variety of clinical improvisation techniques with people who are in pain or distress. They offer a choice of instruments that can be played without prior experience, like drums, rain sticks, hand chimes, xylophones, maracas, and other hand percussion. The players express themselves freely on their instruments or with their voices. The resulting catharsis focuses the players on the creative process and away from their pain or anxiety. Active musical improvisation engages the hands, minds, and emotions of the music makers, flooding their nervous systems with neurotransmitters that inhibit the sensation of pain.

Susan experienced a particularly poignant time while sharing an instrument on the hospice unit.

[8] B. Bittman, L. Berk, and D. Felten, "Composite Effects of Group Drumming Music Therapy on Modulation of Neuroendocrine-Immune Parameters in Normal Subjects," *Alternative Therapy & Health Medicine 7*, no. 1, (2001): 38–47.

I visited Jo, a bed-bound, uncommunicative woman, and placed a tambourine on Jo's belly. I sat beside Jo and quietly began singing the spiritual "Kumbaya" while playing the guitar. To my astonishment, Jo picked up the tambourine and began gently tapping it on the bed rail in time with the music. Her nurse, hearing the sound, quietly entered the room to share the moment. I left the tambourine in the room and later learned that Jo was able to tap the tambourine on the bed rail each time she needed the nurse's attention. A very simple music intervention opened a window of opportunity for Jo to communicate her needs.

Music therapists also utilize a highly specialized methodology that asks an individual to choose a musical instrument to represent pain, and another instrument that is soothing. The person is guided to play out what his or her pain sounds like, and then to gradually introduce soothing sounds. With the therapist's guidance, the individual improvises on these themes, often experiencing dramatic pain relief.[9] These clinical methods can be quite powerful, and therefore, must be practiced with a qualified music therapist. If you are interested in pursuing these and other techniques that require the expertise of a music therapy pain specialist, the American Music Therapy Association[10] and Certification Board for Music Therapists[11] can help you find a qualified professional.

6. Evaluate

Use the Music Plan Worksheet to take notes on your improvisations. You may choose to rate your level of relaxation and/or enjoyment and to comment about your reaction to taking a risk musically. However you choose to experience improvisation, we urge you to play on, let it go, and feel the release through your body, mind, and spirit.

[9] C. Dileo and J. Bradt, "Music Therapy in Stress Management" In *Principles and Practice of Stress Management* (3rd Ed.), eds. P. Lehrer, R. Woolfolk, and W. Sime (New York: Guilford Press, 2007).

[10] www.musictherapy.org

[11] www.cbmt.org

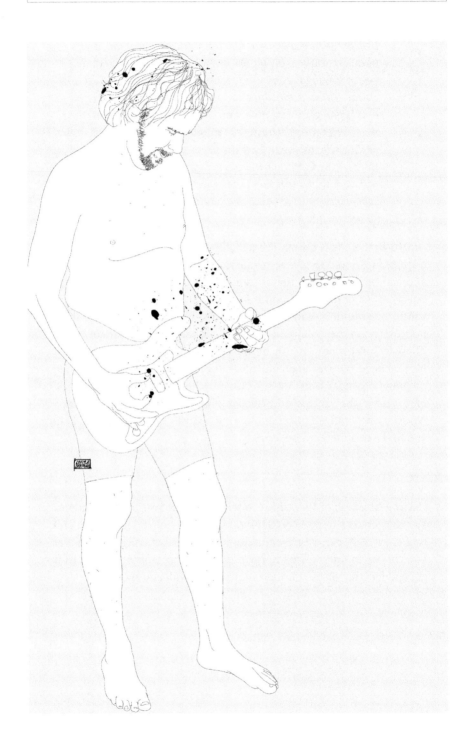

CHAPTER 11

Silence

When dissonance envelops
In a boisterous rush,
I yearn for the silence
Of rhythmic lapping hush.

My thinking becomes muddled.
I grope for clarity.
Bombarded by the noises,
I feel cacophony.

Discord overwhelms me.
I let myself retreat
Deep within my center,
To sense my own heartbeat.

Inhale deeply, soothing air.
Experience the fill.
Slow and steady I exhale.
Calm and quiet, still.

Creativity emerges
As I grow more calm.
My mind is free to wander.
I resonate with song.

As I embrace the peacefulness,
I acknowledge intuition.
Clarity emerges,
I realize decisions.

Apparent is the meaning.
I understand each word.
When I allow my quiet,
"A still small voice is heard."

—Susan E. Mandel

Silence is golden. There are times when we may even crave silence. After all, music seems to follow us everywhere. It traps us in elevators, where we can't escape the sounds. It follows us down supermarket aisles, where it persuades us to linger and buy more food. It provides the atmosphere for a pleasurable dinner out. We can carry it with us on any number of portable music devices.

Sometimes, it is all too much. What we really need is silence. Music must start with silence. The famous pianist Artur Schnabel said, "The notes I handle no better than many pianists. But the pauses between the notes—ah, that is where the art resides." The moments of silence in the music create the suspense, drama, or surprise that give a sense of anticipation and rouse our emotions. Silence can lend meaning to the sounds. No matter how much you enjoy music, silence is also something to appreciate. Knowing when you need the stimulation of music, and when you are overstimulated and require some quiet is a critically important distinction to make.

1. Give Yourself a Dose of Silence

What comes up may surprise you. You may find that your thoughts come flooding in. You may realize how tense your body is feeling. Don't be alarmed if you suddenly sense a wave of emotion. Allow yourself all of these feelings, and welcome them. Sometimes what you need most is a moment to check in and see what is going on inside you. Sometimes you will learn more about yourself or the questions with which you have been grappling when you stop the cycle of stress with a time of silence.

2. Take a Moment to Meditate

There are many forms of meditation. One of the most instinctive ways to meditate is to pay attention to your breath and listen to what is happening around you. If you close your eyes, you can go inward to explore your inner world. Can you feel your heart beating? What do you hear? What do you smell? What are you sensing around you? This is mindfulness meditation. Notice and be mindful of what is happening inside and outside of your body. Notice and be mindful of what is happening in your mind. You will probably find that there are lots of thoughts swimming around in your head. Notice that they are there, let them be, accept them, and then return to your breath. If you find that you are worrying about something, be kind to yourself, acknowledge that you are worrying, and refocus on the life-giving breath that enters and leaves your body.

3. Listen to Music

Perhaps you find that meditation is not your style, yet you yearn for inner quiet. We suggest you listen to relaxing selections from our CD. Try experiencing "Finding Inner Harmony" (track 11), which is intended to guide you to a more relaxed state, or any of the selections on our CD that you find to be relaxing. After the music ends, sit or lie quietly for a few minutes. Experience the silence outside and the quiet within.

4. Evaluate

Use the Music Plan Worksheet to record how you react to moments of silence.

Applications for Everyday Living

Practice makes perfect
You now understand
Try it—Apply it
Success is at hand

—Suzanne B. Hanser

We have introduced you to a constellation of musical experiences. We have asked you to practice the various techniques and see how they affect you. We hope that you have observed changes in your mood and feelings while attempting to work on any stress or pain that you have. If this is the case, then you know that you can take control of how you are feeling by performing one or more of the musical approaches you have learned.

Perhaps you've found that you are cultivating a new musical appetite as you discover music and musical activities that are novel in addition to musical experiences that have sustained you for a long time. Making music more a part of your day may be all you need to improve the quality of your life. In this chapter, we share how people we know are applying our music programs and adapting them to suit their needs when everyday annoyances penetrate their otherwise pleasant demeanors. They are using their ingenuity to find new ways to turn their troubles into triumphs. Based on our own personal histories, we impart some tips for overcoming daily hassles, and tell tales of how music buttresses the day-to-day life of others.

THE TRAFFIC BUSTER

When Suzanne is stuck in traffic on the way to an important appointment, she feels a surge of energy that has no release:

> *I find myself grasping the steering wheel with white knuckles, gritting my teeth, and kicking my left foot. Fortunately, I don't drive a stick shift. Then I turn on my favorite radio station. Suddenly, my fingers unfold to the top ten tunes. I tap the steering wheel in rhythm, providing a percussion section for a familiar song. I sing out, and my teeth show through open lips. My trapped energy feeds the dynamism of the music, and the lyrics come to life with the force of my breath. I release my goal of getting ahead of the car in front of me, and concentrate instead on getting the song right. I pay attention to each word and find new meaning in the singer's message. I am determined to use this idle time to perfect my song and let go of my need to reach my destination. I can't control the cars in front of me, but I can work on my song and work out my tension. If the cars don't move for a few minutes, I can even exercise the kinks in my neck while I sing. Meanwhile, I become mindful of my environment.*

> *While I am confined to my car, I look through the windshield and side windows to turn my awareness away from my inner turmoil, and outward to the surrounding neighborhood. I see whether I can detect something that I never noticed before along this route. I revel in unearthing a bird in a tree, a detail in the architecture of a building, and the stylish fashion of a pedestrian. I sing to the pedestrian even though he can't hear me. When my thoughts return to the frustration of getting nowhere fast, I resume singing and focus on my new goal of learning the song, enjoying the music, and observing the world around myself. I am engaging my senses of hearing, sight, and touch while my mind is still learning lyrics. My anxiety is transformed into amazement at what I can accomplish, and I feel very present.*

THE WORKOUT MOM

Kay, a former triathlete, is mother of two sons under the age of two and is expecting another baby in seven months. Her days are filled with bottles, diapers—and play. But even play can be stressful when there's no time to put her feet up and just relax from morning until night. So Kay arises early, before her babies awaken, to work out. Exercise is the best stress releaser she knows, and her daily training session is energized with upbeat techno and hip-hop music. Kay remarked:

> *The music makes me move faster and keeps me focused on what I'm doing. It keeps me distracted from thoughts of anything else. I put on a good song and turn up the volume on my iPod to push me through to the last sprint. When I'm done, I feel ready for the busy day ahead.*

THE SUBSTITUTE

Grant listens to our CD every day. At work, when he feels like smoking a cigarette, he turns on music instead. When he goes home and has an urge for a martini, he reaches for the CD as an alternative. "The music is addictive, too," he says, "but there are no side effects—just a big change in my mood."

Grant listens straight through. He goes through the breathing exercise, then the workout, the massage, the progressive muscle relaxation, and all of the music and imagery suggestions. If he's interrupted, he starts where he left off. When questioned about the addictive properties of the music, Grant stated:

> *I feel a need for the music, like my cigarettes. But somehow it's different. I crave the music, but it's not a compulsion like it is with cigarettes, and I know it's good for me. As soon as I start the music, my impulse dissipates, and I feel a wave of calm come over me. I don't really need the music. I just like it very, very much.*

THE GUITARIST

Corinne is able to soothe herself when she plays the guitar. Whether it is the repetitive strumming, her instant change of mood, or the attention to her mastery of lovely sounds, she finds that picking up the guitar picks her up in more ways than one. She comments:

To me, stress and distress have many faces. Most often I feel stressed when I'm physically or emotionally tired. I might feel sad, fatigued, or overwhelmed. Whatever the cause, the factor that causes distress is the feeling that I'm not the master of the situation. When I'm not in control, I can't adjust to a change in my circumstances. Throughout my life, I have found that I can manipulate my mood best through music. I have stopped questioning and analyzing the reason why I feel stressed and allowed my emotions to fully shine through music. Very often, I reach for my guitar and give my feelings a melody or a chord progression. I keep strumming and the music somehow answers questions I have never spoken out loud. It is a natural mirror into my soul. I only have to listen to clear my head from anything that just bothered me. It is a great outlet for my stress because music transforms my thoughts into activity. In that way, I burn these "bothering" stress hormones. After a couple of minutes, I feel empowered enough that I'm ready to go again. I solve a lot of problems that way.

THE SINGING BOWL

Singing bowls have been used for thousands of years for meditation and prayer. They come from Tibet and many Asian countries, and are made out of brass, quartz, and other materials. Some claim that they hold magical powers. Kearney finds that striking her singing bowl helps her relax deeply.

When people say that something resonates with them, they usually mean that a thought or feeling rings true or feels right to them. My experience of this also involves an actual physical sensation as well as an awareness. Feeling the vibration of a singing bowl or some other tuned bell designed for meditation practice immediately puts me in a receptive meditative state, both physically and mentally. I can feel my chest resonating or vibrating at the frequency of this bell or bowl. And when we are finally "in tune" with each other, when the oscillating stops and there is just a pure tone, I am calm. In that quiet place, at the end of the breath before I take another, I am present and at peace.

THE CHANTER

Kazunori has a hard time with the pressures of academic deadlines in college. He cannot concentrate when he worries about his exams and papers. Yet chanting recharges him by bringing him inward. He explains:

When I am stressed out at the end of the semester, chanting helps me to create a sense of ease and inner comfort. When I begin chanting, I always start with thanks to external virtues—ancestors, family, friends, creatures, and all nature—in my mind. I focus on my breathing, and my stress seems to move from the inside of my body to the outside. I become fully reassured of my well-being in this world. I repeat the words of the Buddhist Syou-Dai-Gyou tradition I practiced as a child. As I chant, gratitude towards external values shifts to internal ones. I increase my self-awareness of my mind and body, and I can feel my blood circulating throughout my body. My repetitive voice takes me deeply inside to a state of complete serenity.

THE PUNK ROCKER

Dan is turned on by rock music, mostly punk and heavy metal styles. He is also attracted to the electric guitar and synthesizer sounds that accompany industrial noises in the genre known as "industrial rock." Dan is living proof that personal preference is the key to finding the right music to elicit a desirable effect. He describes how listening to this loud, driving music resonates with his mood and moves him beyond. His experience shows the iso-principle in action:

> When I'm feeling down, it's always music I turn to in order to begin to transform my condition into a joyful one. When I can no longer handle how sad or negative I'm feeling, I turn on some very sad music, like Nine Inch Nails' "The Day the Whole World Went Away" from the album Still. I identify with the lyrics, but also the sound of the chords and definitely the precise, throbbing beat and the background sounds. It may take a few more sad songs for me to get tired of my low emotional state. I choose somewhat happier songs to lift me out of my funk. I tend to end up with one of my favorite songs, "I Need More Love" by Robert Randolph and the Family Band. It's very difficult, almost impossible for me to feel low or sad when hearing the song. The words, the rhythm, the whole song brings me up.

THE COMPANION

Susan needs to escape the winter weather because extreme cold adversely affects her health.

> When I leave for a warmer climate, I am often on my own for a prolonged period of time and away from family and friends. When I feel the first pangs of loneliness, I reach for my MP3 player and listen to recordings of musicals. I absorb myself in the lyrics, often singing aloud (and loud!). "On My Own," from

Les Misérables, *might match my gloom, while "If We Only Have Love," from* Jacques Brel Is Alive and Well, *lifts my spirits. "Thank You for the Music" from* Mama Mia *fills me with gratitude. I feel comforted by the memories and meaning that I associate with the words, and the music takes me away from my solitude. I feel the music surround and fill me, and I no longer feel alone.*

A WARM GLOW

Brett shared her experience of listening to music to ease her mental and physical tension before falling asleep at night.

For me, the most stressful time of day is bedtime. I have difficulty relaxing, turning my mind off, and falling asleep. Thoughts and worries race through my mind, from what to wear tomorrow, to what to get at the grocery store, to remembering when to pay the utility bills, all the while counting down the hours until I have to wake up. I've found that sitting in bed and listening to my favorite relaxing music, amid the warm glow of a soft pink lamp, eases my soul and calms my mind. The Velvet Underground's self-titled album brings back happy memories, and the combination of Lou Reed's voice and the repetitive grooves unwind and calm my thoughts. I allow myself to focus on the music and get lost in its trance. Before I know it, tension releases from the face, neck, shoulders, and back. By the time I turn off the music and lights, I feel much more centered and ready to let go of the stresses of the day.

REACHING OUT TO OTHERS

Ellen read an early manuscript of this book, before it was published. She remarked that she recognized how she could reach out to special people in her life with music. One of those people is her dad.

My dad is an amateur magician. He enjoys demonstrating magic tricks to children. On one recent occasion, he shared a card trick with a young boy. After the trick, my dad told the boy that he is ninety years old. The boy's eyes opened wide and he replied, "Wow! You're going to die soon." Although my dad laughed when he told me the story, I thought about how he might really be feeling about the candid remark. It occurred to me that I could help my dad to create a CD of preferred songs to ease the anxiety that often plagues him. And then I began to think about how I can help my pregnant daughter to choose music for listening with her unborn child. I'm beginning to think about music in a new way.

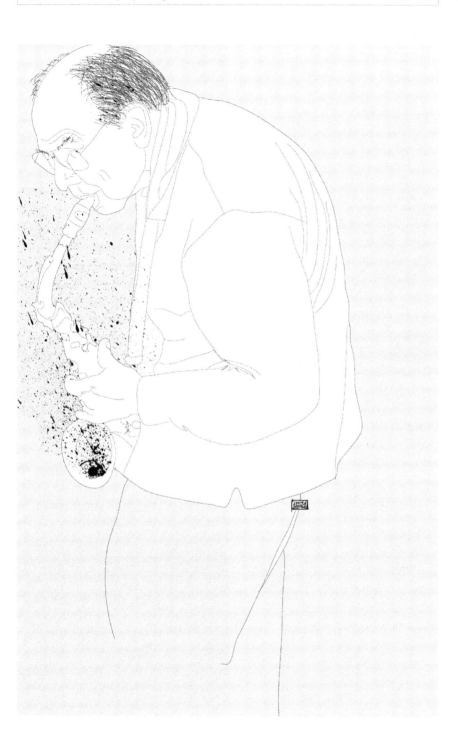

Applications for Stress and Pain

We are all survivors
Traveling our paths
Celebrating life
While working on our tasks
Balance is the key
To look ahead with hope
And live life's lessons one by one
Learning we can cope

—Susan E. Mandel

You are now ready to try adapting our techniques to meet your needs when they matter most. It is one thing to experience these techniques when you are relatively comfortable. It is quite another to be able to apply these methods when you are in pain or under an inordinate amount of stress. Sometimes you will be able to use music well in advance of an expected stressful or painful event—for example, several hours before a job interview or medical procedure. When you have time to prepare, your musical activity can move you into a positive frame of mind that will help you when it counts. If you have practiced regularly, you may find that just listening to the first phrases of the music you sang, played, or heard while practicing will evoke an immediate change in your breathing and heart rate, or your feelings and thoughts. You can actually listen to a recording of the music or you can sing or hum it to yourself. When you begin to feel differently, you know that this music is the prescription that you need at this time.

Each of us experiences challenges through life. We hope that you will find encouragement in some of the remarkable ways that people just like you have used music to manage their most severe challenges. We include a collection of examples here to inspire you to use music when you are confronted with your most serious difficulties.

THE SLEEP MANAGER

Den participated in music therapy after undergoing angioplasty and stent placement—surgical procedures to treat his coronary heart disease. Den retired because his job was highly stressful, and he recognized that his heart rate increased when he felt stressed. Den realized that he was "highly sensitive" and needed to "relax a lot." He noted that he relaxed "head to feet" and that his mind went "blank" when he listened to his music-assisted relaxation and imagery recording. He and his wife listened to the same music each night, applying relaxation and imagery techniques to ease his insomnia (see "Building a Bond with Music," "Finding Inner Harmony," "Sensing Peaceful Images," and "Discovering Your Imagination"). He played the last five minutes of the same music selection upon awakening the following morning.

Den's blank mind and bodily comfort were instrumental in enabling him to release both mental and physical tension, which then allowed him to sleep soundly. Hearing the same music for a few minutes in the morning allowed Den to carry the peaceful feelings that he experienced with the music into the new day.

BRYAN'S LULLABY

Bryan was a spunky five-year-old boy who suffered from insomnia. Alice, Bryan's mother, reported that he "was having difficulty relaxing at night and going to sleep, and staying asleep through the night." Just before Bryan turned three, he underwent brain shunt surgery to relieve large amounts of fluid in his brain. Although the procedure went well with no complications, Bryan began to have sleeping problems.

Alice is a medical receptionist. One day she heard the recording, *Harmony of Mind & Body: A MARI Experience*,[1] playing in the physician's office. This CD combines music with deep breathing, guided relaxation, and guided imagery—the techniques included in chapters 5 and 6. She inquired about the CD and obtained a copy. The first night Alice played the CD for Bryan, she explained to him that it would help him to relax and sleep. Within forty-five minutes of listening, Bryan was asleep. This was in sharp contrast to the two or more hours usually required for Bryan to fall asleep. Equally remarkable to Alice was the fact that Bryan slept through the entire night.

[1] D. Kobialka, and S. E. Mandel, *Harmony of Mind & Body: A MARI Experience,* LiSem Enterprises 108, 2005.

Bryan now listens to his CD regularly at bedtime, and continues to fall asleep within a short time, remaining asleep throughout the night. If Alice does not play this music, Bryan requires over two hours to fall asleep, and reawakens in the middle of the night.

Alice explained:

> *Before I received this CD, I tried everything—lying down with Bryan, rubbing his back, giving him a warm bath before bedtime. Nothing worked! Now my child gets a better night's sleep, and so do I.*

THE PAIN MANAGER

George was about to undergo a lithotripsy procedure to break down a large kidney stone in his left kidney. This was his second kidney stone; the first stone had been treated effectively with lithotripsy. During that first procedure, however, George had a reaction to the anesthetic, and he awakened in the recovery room, shivering and panicked. It took him several minutes to orient to where he was post-surgery, and his blood pressure was dangerously high. He remained in recovery several hours before he was ready to be discharged.

With this second kidney stone, George had been experiencing a great deal of pain. During the night before the lithotripsy procedure, he listened to his relaxing music to help him sleep. Although the music helped him doze, bouts of pain awakened him throughout the long, difficult night. In the morning, his wife brought him to the day surgery unit of their local medical center. George was uncomfortable and unable to lie still. His agitation was making it challenging for the nursing staff to start the IV drip that would sedate him during the lithotripsy. George put on his earphones and turned on his attention-getting music—a medley of Frank Sinatra ballads that he had enjoyed for many years. His agitation immediately subsided, and he fell asleep as the sedative took effect.

The next thing George remembers is waking up in the recovery room. Thanks to his wife's instructions, the surgical nurse had kept George's music playing during the lithotripsy procedure and in recovery. George awakened to the familiar Frank Sinatra CD that he loved. He quickly realized that the procedure was over, and that he was doing well. The ordeal was behind him. Nursing staff commented that George's vital signs were excellent. George noted that awakening to his familiar music gave him a few minutes to orient himself to his surroundings. He did not experience the panic and high blood pressure that occurred after his first procedure. Rather, his immediate response to awakening was the calm and soothing feeling brought on by hearing his favorite music. George was discharged within a couple of hours, without complications or incident.

THE CHRONIC PAIN MANAGER

Pamela suffers from arthritis and osteoporosis. She enjoys listening to music that reminds her of the ocean.

> When I go to the ocean, I lay down in the nice hot sand, and I can feel my whole body and bones feel so good. It's not too hot—the sun is hot but there is a cool breeze coming off the ocean and cooling me, and I feel all the pain go away. That's my place. Sometimes the little birds are walking, or I hear kids. Again, that hot sand just feels so good....

Pamela especially enjoys music that includes the sound of ocean waves. She imagines being on the beach while listening to the music. Then, Pamela is able to appreciate the joy of being by the water without feeling a drop. She turns on her special music, and she is there. It makes a real difference with her symptoms.

> Sometimes when I listen to the CD, it is helping me through a passage back into better health or peace.

SWEET DISTRACTION

Carla was concerned about her upcoming routine colonoscopy. Because she was in her fifties, her physician suggested that she have this procedure to rule out any pathology. Even though Carla does not expect any particular difficulty with this diagnostic test, she tends to get very nervous around medical procedures. She doesn't think that she is afraid of feeling pain. It's just the whole experience of taking her clothes off and feeling vulnerable, then being subjected to an IV start, and finally having an invasive procedure that she would rather not envision. She decided to bring her iPod to the medical center to help distract her from thoughts of the whole experience.

Carla turned on her relaxing playlist after she was prepared for the procedure. She almost fell asleep while she imagined being home in the comfort of her living room. As she was wheeled into the procedure room, she switched to her attention-getting music. She was given conscious sedation and was aware of her surroundings. She breathed along with the rousing song, "We Are Family," and let the repetitive lyrics swarm around in her head. She played the song several times, and then heard her physician call her name, "Carla, you're all done. Everything is fine." Carla sang out "We Are Family" in celebration of the good news and in triumph for getting through a tough day without feeling any discomfort.

THE STRESS MANAGER

Andrew realized that stress was contributing to his cardiac illness. His physicians had warned him for some time that he had to do something about the stress in his life, but he felt powerless to change.

> *I was a super stressful guy. Nothing could help me, because it had to come from within. After listening regularly to the music, I learned how to relax anytime. It helped to reduce stress, and I could do it anywhere. I don't find myself that stressed anymore. Listening to the CD helped me to realize that I have control, rather than outside influences controlling my fluctuations of stress levels. I look at those situations that I get in. I look and see what's going on, and I react a whole lot differently than I used to.*

For Andrew, the first step in managing his stress was to become motivated to help himself. Andrew saw improvement as soon as he began to listen to a music-assisted relaxation and imagery CD. Clearly, practicing the deep breathing, guided relaxation, and imagery enabled him to develop a sense of control over his stress response. Replaying the music and suggestions in his mind helped him to perceive and evaluate changes in his level of stress. He has learned the relaxation skills and puts them to use now whenever he needs them. Because stress is a contributing risk factor for heart disease, Andrew's effective stress management through music is a life-affirming choice.

SLOWING DOWN

Getting a chance to just stay in one spot and listen to something that's slower and wants you to relax makes a big difference. Sometimes I think of things I hadn't thought of for years. I can see things in my mind as I hear the music. By the end of the listening time, I feel very, very calm and just very relaxed. In fact, a couple of times, I fell asleep.

Fred underwent heart surgery at the age of seventy-five. Although he felt "fortunate" that the operation was successful, Fred experienced ongoing anxiety. He commented, "I know it's going to happen eventually for anybody; there will be a time when I won't come back." Fred began to attend music therapy sessions, and received a music recording for home listening that included suggestions for deep breathing, progressive muscle relaxation, and guided imagery. The first time he listened to the CD, Fred remarked that the music and voice were relaxing to him. He listened about three times a week during the first month. Recognizing how much more relaxed he felt after practicing the techniques, he started to play the CD daily. Seven months later, Fred remarked that he no longer suffered from anxiety. His systolic blood pressure dropped ten points with no change in his medication.

FEELING WIGGY

Ida participated in group music therapy after her heart attack. Her stress was associated with adjusting to insulin-dependent diabetes, and she acknowledged, "It is hard to accept the diagnosis of diabetes." Ida described her symptoms of low blood sugar levels as feeling "wiggy." After hearing another group member's story, she recognized that her own upset feelings affected her blood sugar level, and quickly noted the connection between her mind and body. She recognized that she felt panicked and "needlessly worried," when stressed. Ida found that listening to music relaxed her to the point of putting her to sleep. Following one listening experience, Ida described feeling mellow and tranquil, like she was "floating on a cloud." Ida recognized that by listening to her music, she could "handle the stress problems quite a lot." As Ida learned that she was "able to handle everything," she expressed feeling "wiggy" much less often.

THROUGH PAIN AND WILL

Sally lived with unstable angina (chest pain), diabetes, and fibromyalgia. She communicated that she was "on the edge all the time." Sally stated that her life ended at the time of her heart surgery because she had to simplify her life to the point of having "no life."

Then Sally tried music-assisted relaxation and imagery. She felt that this experience enhanced her spirituality. She noted that listening to the recording helped her to cope with insomnia and gave her "strength to deal with the pain" associated with diabetic foot neuropathy, a complication that causes numbness in the feet.

Sally stated, "Energy and how to spend it is a big thing. Stress takes a lot of energy. Relaxation is a slowing down." Sally said that when she listened to her own spiritual music, she felt "more peace." She also remarked, "In my heart, I am a musician. My gift is playing hymns." She discussed her desire to resume playing the piano, but most significant was her discovery that music could help her cope with her pain and restore her will to live.

A NEW WOMAN

Maria was 91 years old and lived at home with her professional care provider. Lately, she had become depressed, and her health was failing. She had always enjoyed classical music, but due to limited mobility, it was hard for her to leave the house to attend concerts. Even though her daughter and son were trained to play violin and trumpet, she herself never had the opportunity to take a lesson. Yet she spoke often about her lifelong desire to play the piano.

For Christmas, her daughter bought her an electronic keyboard, and found a teacher who was able to see Maria at home. Maria immediately took to the instrument. She said, "There is no need to be morose. Playing the keyboard has given me a new lease of life." When she is feeling poorly, her care provider brings over the keyboard. On most days, Maria practices for over an hour, and loves to perform when family and friends come to visit. When she is told that a visitor is expected later in the day, she finds a renewed source of energy to devote to long periods of practice. In the words of her daughter, "The applause brings out her biggest smile, and I see a new woman!"

SHARED JOY

Katherine is caring for her husband, Roosevelt, who has dementia attributed to Alzheimer's disease. They live together in their longtime family home near the center of the city. Katherine finds it more and more challenging to care for Roosevelt, now that he doesn't always recognize her. His condition has been deteriorating, as is expected with a disease such as Alzheimer's, but Katherine is having trouble recalling the things that she always loved about Roosevelt. Recently, he has become angry and unsettled, especially near sunset. "Sundowning" actually refers to symptoms of people with dementia that worsen at the end of the day. This is also the time when Katherine herself is tired and less patient. She will need to prepare their dinner, and Roosevelt will pace around the house, while alternately, mumbling and shouting, sometimes throwing things and punching the air.

Always seeking strategies to shift Roosevelt's attention to something positive, Katherine came upon an idea. She found a songbook that contained a variety of songs that they both loved to sing together at family gatherings. She decided to bring out the songbook every evening, before Roosevelt tended to become agitated. They sat in the living room, and Katherine selected some peppy songs to engage Roosevelt. He particularly enjoyed, "Take Me Out to the Ball Game," "Catch a Falling Star," and "He's Got the Whole World in His Hands." They would start singing, and soon, they were laughing and talking about old times. Roosevelt would still get antsy when Katherine began to prepare dinner, but his mood quickly changed when she began to sing. He joined in and seemingly forgot everything else. This activity was so helpful that Katherine went out to buy some recordings of songs from the fifties and sixties that Roosevelt could listen to when she was otherwise occupied. Listening to music was particularly effective in changing Roosevelt's mood. The singing and music listening gave Katherine and Roosevelt the opportunity to share in a pleasurable activity in which Roosevelt was at his best. During these times, Katherine was relieved to see glimpses of the more cognitively aware Roosevelt whom she so much loved.

THE ENTERTAINER

Jaime is scared stiff of going on stage. He is scheduled to give a concert on Saturday night, but every time he thinks about the music he will be playing, he gets panicky and his heart starts to race. It's not that he is unprepared. He has practiced a long time, and the music is as ready as it can be to be performed. Jaime recognizes that he needs to decondition this music so that he no longer has an automatic panic response to it. So he listens to a piece of music that he has performed successfully at his last concert. Then he imagines himself on stage playing it, free of butterflies in his stomach or a throbbing heart. When he is assured that he can imagine this scene without any anxiety, he moves on to the musical selection he is about to perform. He listens to a recording of his last rehearsal, while he practices two music programs: "A Musical Workout" and "Musical Massage."

He dances playfully in "A Musical Workout," jumping and running around the room while he listens to his music. His intention is to enjoy the experience fully and to begin to associate it with feeling carefree and happy. He imagines himself playing the music as he creates new dance steps. Then he settles into his favorite chair and gives himself a "Musical Massage." As he listens to the music again, he envisions himself performing it. This time, he focuses on the muscles of his face, and works out any tension with his fingertips. He listens one more time while he closes his eyes and pictures himself at the Saturday concert. His body feels relaxed, his mind feels more confident, and he is ready. In the next few days, he repeats these music programs at home and just prior to rehearsal at the performance space. His confidence is building, and he has not experienced the familiar symptoms of performance anxiety. At the concert on Saturday, he takes the stage and masters the music with excitement and elation, as opposed to nervousness and fear. Afterwards, he dances backstage with the same abandon as in "A Musical Workout." Jaime looks forward to his next concert now that he has a more successful experience of performing behind him, and some effective ways to prepare himself emotionally.

IN A MOTHER'S WORDS:
A PRE- AND POST-NATAL MUSIC LISTENING EXPERIENCE

Dee discovered that she was expecting a baby at the beginning of her graduate studies in mathematics education. With a scholar's curiosity, she embarked on a musical experiment. She began to listen to music nightly during her sixth month of pregnancy. Dee described her plan in a mathematician's exacting terms:

> From the Baby's First: Classics CD (Volume I), I first played Beethoven's Moonlight Sonata, which was 7 minutes and 42 seconds, followed by Brahms' "Lullaby," which was only 2 minutes and 2 seconds. I selected the Beethoven piece just because I enjoyed listening to it and it had a variety of musical sounds for the little one to hear. Since this version of the Brahms piece was so brief, I played it twice each evening. Brahms' "Lullaby" was a natural choice as a final song before bedtime for the baby.

Dee described her own reaction to the nightly music listening:

> *My major gain from listening to the music was relaxation. Having taught high school math daily for seven hours, along with all the activities that come along with preparing for a little one's arrival, I was generally exhausted by the end of each day. The twelve minutes of music and relaxation helped clear my mind and prepare me for a good night's sleep without my mind racing about the next days' coming events.*

Although the unborn baby's activity varied during music listening, Dee remarked about the baby's consistent response to each musical piece:

> *During the* Moonlight Sonata, *she would either remain active if she had been awake and moving at the start, or if she had been still she would wake up and begin moving in response to the music. I often changed the position of the speaker with respect to my tummy (left, right, or middle). Many times she would orient herself toward the direction from where the music was being played. In fact, several times when I would lay the speaker directly on my tummy, she would kick the speaker from inside during the low bass notes in the* Moonlight Sonata. *I am not sure if it was the vibrations that caused her to react or actually hearing the note itself, but she very frequently located and kicked the exact location of the speaker during that song. And the speaker was very lightweight so I knew the reaction was not from her feeling squashed! During Brahms' "Lullaby," her activity from the first song slowly faded to gentle rolling, and by the end of the second playing of this piece every night, she was completely still. I found it amazing that her reaction to "Lullaby" was so consistent, as sometimes she was being quite active when I began to play this selection, and yet by the end, she was quiet and still.*

Dee continued playing music until her delivery day. She resumed music listening after bringing her baby girl home from the hospital.

I played both songs consecutively while rocking my daughter to sleep each evening for the first few months of her life. Her reaction was not as noticeable to the Moonlight Sonata, *as she continued to do whatever she was doing when the piece began (cooing, playing with her fingers, etc.). Her reaction to "Lullaby" was amazing, though. Each time it started, she would hold perfectly still and turn her gaze toward the CD player. It was almost as though she recognized the song and was having a repeat performance of her reaction to that song prior to delivery. I tested her to see if she was just responding to slow, quiet music by playing other slow, quiet songs, but she did not show any signs of recognizing them. It was truly miraculous to watch.*

When asked if she recommended that other expectant mothers listen to music, Dee replied affirmatively and enthusiastically:

This experience was absolutely incredible. Not only did it provide me the relaxation I needed at the end of long days of pregnancy, it created a medium through which I could communicate with my growing baby prior to delivery. I expected to interact with my baby once she arrived, but being able to see the signs of deliberate communication on her part before birth was astonishing! And watching her seeming recognition of the music after delivery made me cry. This experience made me feel as though I was connecting with her emotionally before I could hold her physically. Truly a blessing!

AMAZING GRACE

Ruth and Jean were the best of friends. They enjoyed singing together in their church choir. Ruth was singing in church one Sunday morning when she collapsed in pain. She was rushed to the hospital, where a doctor told her that she required emergency surgery to remove one of her kidneys. The doctor explained to Ruth that she might not survive. Immediately following the surgery, Ruth suffered a massive stroke and remained unconscious for several days.

When Jean came to visit at the hospital, Ruth was in a comatose state and Jean knew that her beloved friend was near death. She gently stroked Ruth's arm, and tearfully and quietly sang "He's Got the Whole World in His Hands" and "Amazing Grace." As she said goodbye to Ruth, Jean knew in her heart that Ruth heard her singing.

The following morning when Jean called the hospital to check on her friend, she was informed that Ruth awoke from the coma. Jean learned that the only thing that Ruth recalled was hearing an "angel singing." It seemed that the singing called her back. With time and therapy, Ruth fully recovered. During a choir rehearsal two months later, Ruth shared a memory of her experience.

> I started hearing this music, my favorite song, "Amazing Grace." It felt good, but I did not know if I was alive or not because it felt so good. But I liked it. The next thing I remember was hearing someone say, "You're fine... they removed your kidney."

Jean asked Ruth to sing "Amazing Grace" along with the choir. Disregarding her speech impairment, Ruth sang the hymn from her heart and soul. Everyone present that day can attest to the power of music.

THE EASY LISTENER

We sent our CD to our friend Suzy when she took a fall and broke two ribs. She told us about the impact it had on her and shared her thoughts on some of her favorite pieces:

> I played the CD continuously from morning until night. I played it while I slept. It was my constant companion during some very difficult times punctuated by constant terrible pain. I could have felt lonely, dashed, and sorry for myself, but these pieces held my spirit high, and instilled within me a pulsating joy. I never was in a position before in my life where I had to be that still. Breathing hurt. I concentrated on the notes, the progression, the silence between the notes, the beginning of a piece and the ending. I lived the notes one by one into healing. I am grateful beyond words for the stepping stones that led me to the gentle cessation of pain. In that sense, as in everything that befalls us, it was pure blessing and grace.

Suzy commented about several musical selections from the CD:

- "Bonsai"

> This piece helped me stay inside my body, to go within, even though that is where the pain was. I sent light to my broken ribs and let the tinkling vibratory notes penetrate and heal me. This had a soothing effect on my nervous system as well. This piece instructed me that the pain would leave.

- "Traumerai"

> The very slow tempo of this piano piece helped me stay in the present moment of my slow life. Off the bike, off the running path, off to the side. Sitting, being still, healing. I would play this every morning and let the slow unfolding of the notes act as a metronome for my new pace. Snail's pace. This way I could be reminded

to stay in touch with everything that was quiet and still within me, including the pain. This piece led me by the hand when no one else was there beside me. Thus, I never, ever felt alone.

- "Sequoia"

  This piece quieted my mind of fear. Each tone was like a golden drop of light that penetrated my brokenness. I tried to hear the gaps between the notes, and breathe (as much as I could breathe), and know that as one note stopped, there was space in between and there I could just BE. In one sense, having to be still and not partake of the world outside my door was a huge relief. This insight was revelatory to me.

- "To a Wild Rose"

  I played piano when I was a child, and this piece was one of my favorites. Listening to it took me back to my youth. I envisioned my fingers on the keys. I meditated on each solitary note. I walked along on them and let that journey take me wherever it wanted to. I imagined myself in my mother's arms as a baby—enfolded, safe, secure. This brought my body into more harmony and banished stressful thoughts that I would never be okay again.

- "Gymnopedie #1"

  This music and imagery brought me to a scene from The Bridges of Madison County. *I played the movie in my mind. I left my place, body, mind, and was in the kitchen with Meryl Streep and Clint Eastwood. This brought back the memory of early loves in my life, and how that love remains to this day. That I could use my memories of those times as a field in which to stand showed me that love and tenderness heals all.*

- "Clair de Lune"

  Evening is when I most enjoyed this piece. I was saying goodbye to another day of my life spent sitting, meditating, reading, talking with friends who would stop by, looking out the window at the life that wasn't mine anymore. This piece gave me permission and support to be slow, sedentary, quiet, humble, and still.

YOUR MUSIC APPLICATIONS

Can you relate to any of these stories? Have you had similar experiences? Are there adaptations you can make to these examples so that they help you directly? Do these people inspire you to incorporate music into your life in new and different ways? Like the new mother Dee, we hope you will celebrate life with music, in addition to applying it when you are in stress or pain.

When and where will you next use your personal music plan? We encourage you to make music a part of your life and enjoy yourself!

PART III:
Evaluate and Enhance Your Music Plan

CHAPTER 14

Coda: Music for Life

"Music: An Overture to Connection"

Welcome the hush, embrace the still
With quiet music the silence fills
Symphony in nature, chorus of sounds
Drone of wind's sigh, bird tunes resound
Rat-a-tat-tat of puppy's paws
Echo of chimes, crow's brass caw-caw's
Sense the vibration around and within
Physical presence, welcome it in
Absorb the sounds in harmony
Open wide to infinity
Now sing with the chorus, at one with each part
Blending together of voices and hearts
I open my mouth to let the sound through
Convey my music, my rhythm, my tune
Music is energy—I feel connected
Intense pleasure, moment perfected
Sensation pierces to deep within
Reaches my spirit, I welcome it in
Exquisite music, express my soul's speech
I profoundly receive it, as outward I reach

—Susan E. Mandel

We have asked a great deal from you. We have told you all sorts of things you can do with music. We have given you a recording of music with more suggestions of things to do. Perhaps you have tried out the music programs we described, perhaps you haven't. We hope that you listened to our CD, but perhaps you didn't. It is time to do very little more, but simply to reflect on what you have read and heard, and see what seems right for you.

EVALUATE YOUR EXPERIENCES

Now that we have familiarized you with our ideas, you are ready to decide how music can enhance your life. You have the tools to develop your own personal music plan. If you have been keeping a Music Listening Log, you have documented the effects that certain pieces of music have on you. You may also know which music programs have had the most impact on your stress and pain. If you have been noting your relaxation and enjoyment of the music programs in the Music Plan Worksheet, you should have an idea of the most influential music and music programs. But if you haven't been keeping notes, you can still use your experience as your guide in planning ahead. Of course, you may choose not to engage in a formal plan, but rather simply continue to listen to your favorite music when it is convenient. Alternatively, you can summarize and evaluate your experiences with music to determine if you wish to change your music habits or take on a new creative challenge. However you use our book and CD, we hope that you are realizing how music affects you and loving the entire experience.

COMMIT TO YOUR PLAN

We hope that you have witnessed the positive impact of several different music techniques. Based on your experiences and the practical realities of undertaking our music programs, only you know when and how you can implement these techniques. If you develop a plan, we think you have a better chance of augmenting your musical life while coping with your stress and pain. But we acknowledge that committing to a plan may be challenging.

As an incentive, many people find it helpful to develop a contract that delineates a schedule for engaging in the music activities. This agreement serves to concretize your commitment to participate in some music experiences on a regular basis. This document can be as uncomplicated as single written statements, like: "I agree to listen to my special music once a day at _:_ o'clock," or "I will take a piano lesson once a week, and practice one-half hour, four days per week, at _:_ o'clock." It could simply be a notation in your daily calendar to remind yourself to listen to some music or practice one of the techniques. Perhaps you want to tack a reminder note to yourself on your bulletin board or set an alert on your personal digital assistant (if your appointments are on a mobile phone or device). The contract can be solely an agreement with yourself, or you could call in a witness who co-signs and supports your commitment.

Setting an easily achievable goal is important to ensure that you set yourself up for success. It is far better to set out a goal that you are confident you can meet rather than letting yourself down. If you find yourself not meeting the expectations of your plan, re-evaluate and substitute some small steps towards reaching your goal. While we urge you to be realistic, we are also asking you to stretch your creative potential, and take a risk to try something you haven't done before. Only you know the balance between these forces that enables you to feel good.

VALUE YOURSELF

What's important? Your values and your value. We have emphasized that treating yourself to music is one way of taking care of yourself and caring for yourself. Taking care of yourself means doing things that are good for you. Now is the time to take charge of making some positive changes in your life. Caring for yourself means respecting the way you are, accepting both your strengths and weaknesses, and allowing yourself to experience the beauty and joy in life. It means being kind to yourself, showing patience as you try something different, and giving yourself a break. Sometimes we are our own worst enemies. We don't treat ourselves with compassion as we would a friend. We may have higher standards or greater expectations for our performance than for anyone else's, and we criticize or punish ourselves as we would never treat another person. If you are ready to take care of and care for yourself, we believe that you will benefit greatly from using the music programs described in this book.

Embrace the beautiful music that is currently in your life by giving it more playing time in your day. Now is the moment of truth. Are you convinced that taking this time for yourself may be helpful to you? Do you believe that you deserve this opportunity for self-care? Commit to making music more a part of your life. You determine the parameters and the process. You set the conditions for making changes that can enhance the quality of your life. It is up to you to determine whether a contract or schedule is right for you. What is important is that you make time to implement what works for you. We believe that, through experiencing the myriad ways of listening to, singing, playing, improvising, and learning music, you will discover that you can manage stress and pain throughout your life, while bringing a new, creative dimension to living.

Move through stress and pain
Let music resound within
Life begins anew

—Suzanne B. Hanser and Susan E. Mandel

ACKNOWLEDGMENTS

The swimmer kicks with unusual strength,
Strokes with all of her might.
Moves in rhythm, at one with the water,
Knows the end is in sight.
Miles behind her, her task is complete.
Aware that it's time to move on,
Still she reaches for one last lap.
Knows that this chapter is done.
She exits the water. Breathes in deeply
Insight of clarity and light.
This last lap in truth a beginning.
The next pool is just out of sight.

—Susan E. Mandel

We are both swimmers, and we love to immerse ourselves in aquatic metaphors. There are many people who have kept this book afloat, and so we take this opportunity to acknowledge their contributions.

We are flowing with gratitude—for being given the gift of music, for being able to share our experience with you, and for having the opportunity to collaborate. In our effort to acknowledge people who have helped us bring our work to you, our readers, we recognize that our many supporters are too numerous to mention.

We are bathed in the love of our families, and they have been at our side as we undertook the challenge to publish a book and CD out of our experiences. Our spouses, Alan Teperow and Dr. Martin Mandel, stood on the shore, cheering us on.

The people who have shared their musical experiences in this book have buoyed us—with awe at the power of music in their lives. Each one has been a teacher, sharing unique lessons of life with music and music therapy. We recognize the countless number of people who have worked with us and whose insights prepared us to write this book.

Anita Louise Steele and Herbert Strawbridge (of blessed memory), from the Kulas Foundation, recognized that together, we could dive into uncharted waters—complementing each other's experience and expertise. They introduced us to each other as research collaborators, knowing that the sum of our contributions would be greater than that which each of us could accomplish alone. We thank Cynthia Moore-Hardy, CEO and president of Lake Health, for her vision and ongoing support of music therapy and our research efforts.

Berklee Press and Hal Leonard Corporation allowed us to dip our toes into a music self-help book, taking a risk on a new genre of music resources. We thank our editor, Jonathan Feist.

Louisa Bertman took the plunge with us and provided her beautiful illustrations to put our words into motion.

Chee-Ping Ho and Rob Jaczko guided our strokes and mixed our words and music into a CD for your enjoyment.

Daniel Kobialka has been our kickboard as we glided through our own stress and pain with the most beautiful music we could find and discovered his magnificent arrangements and original creations. Daniel's music not only inspired our music programs, but also motivated us to research the impact of his music on others. We are grateful to include two of his contributions on our CD.

The music therapy students at Berklee College of Music rode the waves of confidence and questioning with us, as they embarked on their own careers as music therapists. Their passion for music captured our hearts and moved us to write this book.

Brett Collins and Marcia Klein swam alongside, reading drafts to ensure our clarity.

And lastly, you, our readers, have jumped into the water with us, with faith that we have something to offer you. We thank you for the trust you have placed in us to guide you to improved wellness with music.

Musically yours,

Suzanne B. Hanser

Susan Emandel

Bibliography, Music Resources, and For Further Reading

BIBLIOGRAPHY

American Heart Association. "Risk Factors and Coronary Heart Disease," 2009, http://www.americanheart.org/presenter.jhtml?identifier=4726.

American Music Therapy Association, http://musictherapy.org/

Association for Music and Imagery, http://www.ami-bonnymethod.org/general_info_gim.asp

Benson, H. *The Relaxation Response*. New York: HarperTorch, 1975.

Benson, H., and W. Proctor, *The Breakout Principle*. New York: Scribner, 2003.

Bittman, B., L. Berk, D. Felten, et al. "Composite Effects of Group Drumming Music Therapy on Modulation of Neuroendocrine-Immune Parameters in Normal Subjects." *Alternative Therapy & Health Medicine* 7, no. 1 (2001): 38-47.

Bonny, H.L. and L.M. Savary. *Music and Your Mind: Listening with a New Consciousness*. Barrytown, New York: Station Town Press, 1990.

Burns, D.D. *The Feeling Good Handbook*. New York, NY: Plume, 1999.

Certification Board for Music Therapists, http://cbmt.org/

Csikszentmihaly, M. *Flow: The Psychology of Optimal Experience*. New York: Harper & Row, 1990.

Dileo, C., and J. Bradt. "Music Therapy in Stress Management." In *Principles and Practice of Stress Management* (3rd Ed.), edited by P. Lehrer, R. Woolfolk, and W. Sime, New York: Guilford Press, 2007.

Gatewood, E.L. "The Psychology of Music in Relation to Anesthesia." *American Journal of Surgery, Anesthesia Supplement* 35 (1921): 47–50.

Hanser, S. B. "Childbirth, Childdeath." In *Educators, Therapists, and Artists on Reflective Practice*, edited by J.J.G. Byers and M. Forinash, New York: Peter Lang, 2004.

Hanser, S. B., S. Bauer-Wu, L. Kubicek, M. Healey, J. Manola, M. Hernandez, and C. Bunnell. "Effects of a Music Therapy Intervention on Quality of Life and Distress in Women with Metastatic Breast Cancer." *Journal of the Society for Integrative Oncology* 5, no. 1 (2006), 14–23.

Hanser, S. B., J. Butterfield-Whitcomb, M. Kawata, and B.E. Collins. "Home-Based Music Strategies with Individuals Who Have Dementia and Their Family Caregivers." Pending publication.

Hanser, S. B., S. C. Larson, and A. S. O'Connell. "The Effect of Music on Relaxation of Expectant Mothers During Labor," *Journal of Music Therapy* 20, no. 2 (1983): 50–58.

Hanser, S. B., and L. W. Thompson. "Effects of a Music Therapy Strategy on Depressed Older Adults." *Journal of Gerontology* 49, no. 6 (1994): 265–269.

Holden, S. "From Death's Door to Earning the Keys to the World," *New York Times*, October 14, 2009, http://www.nytimes.com/2009/10/15/arts/music/15gardot.html.

Kobialka, D., http://www.wonderofsound.com

Kreutz, G., S. Bongard, S. Rohrmann, V. Hodapp, and D. Grebe. "Effects of Choir Singing or Listening on Secretory Immunoglobulin A, Cortisol, and Emotional State." *Journal of Behavioral Medicine* 27, no. 6 (2004): 623–635.

Mandel, S. E. "Music Therapy: A Personal Peri-Surgical Experience." *Music Therapy Perspectives* 5 (1988): 109–110.

Mandel, S. E., S. B. Hanser, and L. J. Ryan. "Effects of a Music-Assisted Relaxation and Imagery Compact Disc Recording on Health-Related Outcomes in Cardiac Rehabilitation." *Music Therapy Perspectives* 28, no. 1 (2010): 11–21.

Mandel, S. E., S. B. Hanser, M. Secic, and B. A. Davis. "Effects of Music Therapy on Health-Related Outcomes in Cardiac Rehabilitation: A Randomized Controlled Trial." *Journal of Music Therapy* 44, no. 3 (2007), 176–197.

Maslow, A. *Religion, Values and Peak Experiences.* New York: Viking, 1970.

Melzack, R. "Pain and the Neuromatrix in the Brain." *Journal of Dental Education* 65 (2001): 1378–1382.

Melzack, R., and P. D. Wall. "Pain Mechanisms: A New Theory." *Science* 150 (1965): 971–979.

Montello, L. *Essential Musical Intelligence.* Wheaton, IL: Quest Books, 2002.

Stefano, G. B., B.T. Fricchione, B.T. Slingsby, and H. Benson. "The Placebo Effect and the Relaxation Response: Neural Processes and Their Coupling to Constitutive Nitric Oxide." *Brain Research Reviews* 35 (2001): 1–19.

Sterling, P., and J. Eyer. "Allostasis: A New Paradigm to Explain Arousal Pathology." In *Handbook of Life Stress, Cognition and Health,* edited by S. Fisher & J. Reason, New York: John Wiley & Sons, 1988.

MUSIC RESOURCES

GarageBand, http://www.garageband.com

Guitar Hero, http://www.hub.guitarhero.com

Jam Studio, http://www.jamstudio.com/Studio/index.htm

Kobialka, D., & S. E. Mandel, (2005). "Harmony of Mind & Body: A MARI Experience," *Wonder of Sound,* 2009, http://www.wonderofsound.com

Mixcraft, www.acoustica.com/mixcraft

Noteflight. http://www.noteflight.com/login

Piano Teacher Resources. http://www.netrover.com/~kingskid/piano/piano.html

Play! Making Tracks, http://www.bbc.co.uk/orchestras/play

Rock Band, http://www.rockband.com

Subotnick, M. Creating Music, http://www.creatingmusic.com

Tony-b Machine, http://www.tony-b.org

Wii Music, http://www.wiimusic.com

FOR FURTHER READING

Benson, H. *Timeless Healing: The Power and Biology of Belief.* New York, NY: Scribner, 1996.

Carlson, R. *Don't Sweat the Small Stuff...And It's All Small Stuff.* New York, NY: Hyperion, 2008.

Coates, T.J., and C. E. Thoreson. *How to Sleep Better: A Drug-Free Program for Overcoming Insomnia.* Englewood Cliffs, NJ: Prentice-Hall, 1977.

Crandall, J. *Self-Transformation Through Music.* Wheaton, IL: Theosophical Publishing House, 1988.

Davis, M., M. McKay, and E. R. Eshelman. *The Relaxation and Stress Reduction Workbook* (2nd ed.). Oakland, CA: New Harbinger, 1982.

Davis, W. B., K. E. Gfeller, and M. H. Thaut. *An Introduction to Music Therapy: Theory and Practice* (3rd ed.). Silver Spring, MD: The American Music Therapy Association, 2008.

Hanser, S. B. *The New Music Therapist's Handbook* (2nd ed.). Boston, MA: Berklee Press, 1999.

Jampolsky, M.D., G.G. *Love Is Letting Go of Fear.* Milbrae, CA: Celestial Arts, 1979.

Jourdain, R. (1997). *Music, the Brain, and Ecstasy.* New York, NY: William Morrow.

Juslin, P, and J. Sloboda. *The Handbook of Music and Emotion.* Oxford, UK: Oxford University Press, 2009.

LeDoux, J. *The Emotional Brain: The Mysterious Underpinnings of Emotional Life.* New York, NY: Touchstone, Simon & Schuster, 1996.

Lehrer, P. M., R. L. Woolfolk, and W. E. Sime. *Principles and Practice of Stress Management* (3rd ed.). New York, NY: The Guilford Press, 2007.

Levitin, D.J. *This is Your Brain on Music.* New York, NY: Plume, 2007.

Levkoff, S. E., Y. K. Chee, and S. Noguchi. *Aging in Good Health: Multidisciplinary Perspectives.* New York, NY: Springer, 2001.

Lewinsohn, P.M., R.F. Munoz, M. A. Youngren, and A. M. Zeiss. *Control Your Depression.* Englewood Cliffs, NJ: Prentice-Hall, 1978.

Lewis, Z.A. *I Hope They Know: The Essential Handbook on Alzheimer's Disease and Care.* College Station, TX: Virtualbookworm.com, 2008.

Looker, T., and O. Gregson. *Managing Stress.* Blacklick, OH: McGraw-Hill, 2008.

Mathieu, W.A. *The Listening Book: Discovering Your Own Music.* Boston, MA: Shambhala, 1991.

Monat, A., and R. Lazarus. *Stress and Coping.* New York, NY: Columbia University Press, 1991.

Murdock, M. *Spinning Inward: Using Guided Imagery with Children for Learning, Creativity and Relaxation.* Boston, MA: Shambhala, 1987.

O'Hara, V. *Five Weeks to Healing Stress: The Wellness Option.* Oakland, CA: New Harbinger, 1996.

Ornstein, R., and D. Sobel. *Healthy Pleasures.* Woburn, MA: Addison-Wesley, 1989.

Pincus, D., and A. A. Sheikh. *Imagery for Pain Relief.* New York, NY: Taylor & Francis, 2009.

Polsky, M.E. *Let's Improvise: Becoming Creative, Expressive and Spontaneous through Drama.* Englewood Cliffs, NJ: Prentice-Hall, 1980.

Rothenberg, D. *Why Birds Sing: A Journey into the Mystery of Bird Song.* New York, NY: Basic Books, 2005.

Sacks, O. *Musicophilia.* New York, NY: Knopf, 2007.

Sapolsky, R. M. *Why Zebras Don't Get Ulcers: The Acclaimed Guide to Stress, Stress-Related Diseases, and Coping.* New York, NY: Henry Holt & Co., 2004.

Schneck, D. J., and D. S. Berger. *The Music Effect: Music Physiology and Clinical Applications*. London, UK: Jessica Kingsley, 2006.

Sloboda, J. A. *The Musical Mind: The Cognitive Psychology of Music*. New York: Oxford University Press, 1997.

Storr, A. *Music and the Mind*. New York, NY: Random House, 1992.

Strauss, S. *Inner Rhythm: An Exciting New Approach to Stress-Free Living*. San Francisco, CA: Chase, 1985.

Stroebe, W., and M. S. Stroebe. *Bereavement and Health: The Psychological and Physical Consequences of Partner Loss*. Cambridge, UK: Cambridge University Press, 1987.

Szasz, T. *Pain and Pleasure: A Study of Bodily Feelings* (2nd expanded ed.). Syracuse, NY: Syracuse University Press, 1988.

Volicer, L., and L. Bloom-Charette. *Enhancing the Quality of Life in Advanced Dementia*. Philadelphia, PA: Taylor & Francis, 1999.

Weintraub, M., and M. S. Micozzi. *Alternative and Complementary Treatment in Neurologic Illness*. Philadelphia, PA: Churchill, Livingstone, 2001.

Wigram, T., and J. De Backer. *Clinical Applications of Music Therapy in Psychiatry*. London, UK: Jessica Kingsley, 1999.

Wigram, T., B. Saperston, and R. West. *The Art and Science of Music Therapy: A Handbook*. The Netherlands: Hardwood Academic Publishers, 1996.

Log Sheets

Feel free to copy these log sheets for your personal use, as you work through the exercises discussed in this book.

- Stress Assessment Log

- Pain Assessment Log

- Music Listening Log

- Music Plan Worksheet

Stress Assessment Log
Rating Scale

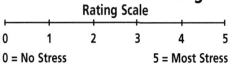

```
0     1     2     3     4     5
```

0 = No Stress   5 = Most Stress

Date 1:_____   Date 2:_____

Describe your stress   **Stress Rating**

List stressful events   Date 1   Date 2

1. _____   _____   _____

2. _____   _____   _____

3. _____   _____   _____

4. _____   _____   _____

5. _____   _____   _____

6. _____   _____   _____

Describe how you feel tension in your body.

Rate your bodily tension.

	Date 1	Date 2		Date 1	Date 2
• Head and Face	_____	_____	• Muscles (central)	_____	_____
• Neck	_____	_____	• Legs	_____	_____
• Hands	_____	_____	• Knees	_____	_____
• Arms	_____	_____	• Feet and Ankles	_____	_____
• Shoulders	_____	_____	• Other	_____	_____
• Back	_____	_____			

Describe your thoughts.

Stressful Events   Date 1 Thoughts   Date 2 Thoughts

1. _____   _____   _____
   _____   _____   _____
   _____   _____   _____
   _____   _____   _____

2. _____   _____   _____
   _____   _____   _____
   _____   _____   _____
   _____   _____   _____

3. _____   _____   _____
   _____   _____   _____
   _____   _____   _____
   _____   _____   _____

4. _____   _____   _____
   _____   _____   _____
   _____   _____   _____
   _____   _____   _____

5. _____   _____   _____
   _____   _____   _____
   _____   _____   _____
   _____   _____   _____

6. _____   _____   _____
   _____   _____   _____
   _____   _____   _____
   _____   _____   _____

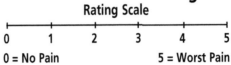

Pain Assessment Log
Rating Scale

| 0 | 1 | 2 | 3 | 4 | 5 |

0 = No Pain   5 = Worst Pain

Part 1: Rate your bodily pain.   Date: _____

Pain Rating   Pain Rating

- Head and Face _____
- Neck _____
- Hands _____
- Arms _____
- Shoulders _____
- Back _____

- Muscles (central) _____
- Legs _____
- Knees _____
- Feet and Ankles _____
- Other _____

Part 2: Describe your pain

- Constant or intermittent
- Cold or hot
- Other

- Sharp or dull
- Focused in one area or diffused

_____

_____

_____

_____

_____

_____

_____

Part 3: How and when does your pain change?

• During and after activities (walking, exercising, singing, etc.)   During   After

_____   _____   _____

_____   _____   _____

_____   _____   _____

_____   _____   _____

• During and after quiet times (reading, music listening, etc.)   During   After

_____   _____   _____

_____   _____   _____

_____   _____   _____

_____   _____   _____

• Other distractions   During   After

_____   _____   _____

_____   _____   _____

_____   _____   _____

_____   _____   _____

Part 4: What increases and what eases your pain?

_____

_____

_____

_____

_____

_____

_____

Music Listening Log

Rating Scale

0   1   2   3   4   5

0 = None   5 = Most

Date: _____

Playlists (categories)

A. *Attention focusing*

B. *Energizing*

C. *Relaxing*

D. *Sleep inducing*

E. *Spiritual*

F. *Other* _____

G. *Leftovers*

Favorite Music Selections:

• Music with happy memories	Rate Relaxation	Rate Enjoyment	Playlist
Childhood _____	_____	_____	_____
_____	_____	_____	_____
_____	_____	_____	_____
_____	_____	_____	_____
Teenage years _____	_____	_____	_____
_____	_____	_____	_____
_____	_____	_____	_____
_____	_____	_____	_____
Television, movies, concerts _____	_____	_____	_____
_____	_____	_____	_____
_____	_____	_____	_____
_____	_____	_____	_____
Relationships _____	_____	_____	_____
_____	_____	_____	_____
_____	_____	_____	_____
_____	_____	_____	_____

From *Manage Your Stress and Pain Through Music*

Milestones, celebrations _____ _____ _____ _____

_____ _____ _____ _____

_____ _____ _____ _____

_____ _____ _____ _____

Vacations _____ _____ _____ _____

_____ _____ _____ _____

_____ _____ _____ _____

_____ _____ _____ _____

Religious or spiritual occasions_____ _____ _____ _____

_____ _____ _____ _____

_____ _____ _____ _____

_____ _____ _____ _____

Recent listening _____ _____ _____ _____

_____ _____ _____ _____

_____ _____ _____ _____

_____ _____ _____ _____

Match your music

	Playlist		**Playlist**
Good morning	_____	*Painful encounters*	_____
Off to work	_____	*Bedtime*	_____
Household chores	_____	*Weekends*	_____
Time to unwind	_____	*Travel*	_____
Stressful moments	_____	*Other*	_____

Music Plan Worksheet
Rating Scale

```
|-------|-------|-------|-------|-------|
0       1       2       3       4       5
```

0 = None   5 = Most

Date: _____

Program	Musical Selection	Relaxation	Enjoyment
• Take a Deep Breath	_____	_____	_____
• A Musical Workout	_____	_____	_____
• Musical Massage	_____	_____	_____
• Building a Bond with Music	_____	_____	_____
• Finding Inner Harmony	_____	_____	_____
• Sensing Peaceful Images	_____	_____	_____
• Discovering Your Imagination	_____	_____	_____
• Focus Your Attention	_____	_____	_____
• Creative Problem Solving	_____	_____	_____
• Lullaby and Good Night	_____	_____	_____
• A Musical Boost	_____	_____	_____
• Singing	_____	_____	_____
• Chanting	_____	_____	_____
• Songwriting	_____	_____	_____
• Playing an Instrument	_____	_____	_____
• Improvising	_____	_____	_____
• Silence	_____	_____	_____

From *Manage Your Stress and Pain Through Music*

Which programs helped you to manage your stress or pain? _____

_____

_____

_____

_____

_____

_____

_____

_____

_____

_____

_____

_____

_____

_____

_____

_____

_____

_____

_____

_____

INDEX

clinical, 110–11
evaluation of, 111
goals v., 108
group, 110
Hanser on, 108
with music therapist, 110–11
pain and, 111
on piano, 108
rhythm and, 107–8
singing and, 109
industrial rock, 122
*Inner Rhythm: An Exciting New
Approach to Stress-Free Living*
(Strauss), 160
insomnia, 128–29, 133
instrumental music, 70
instruments, musical. *See also*
specific types
acoustic, 105
choosing, 104–5
electronic, 104–5, 134
evaluation of learning, 106
guitar, 120
lessons, 105–6
playing, 103–6
risk and, 104–6
interactions, 78
*An Introduction to Music Therapy:
Theory and Practice*
(Davis, W. B.), 158
inwardness, 92
iso-principle, 84, 122
iTunes, 41
"I've Been Working on the
Railroad," 99

J
Jacobson, Edmond, 62
Jacques Brel Is Alive and Well, 123
Jampolsky, M. D., 158
JamStudio, 100, 157
jaw massage, 59–61
jazz, 110
Jourdain, R., 158

journal, 26, 70, 91, 96
Juslin, P., 158

K
Kawata, M., 156
kidney stones, 129
Kobialka, Daniel, xviii, 8, 67, 68,
71–73, 82, 156, 157
Kreutz, G., 156
Kubicek, Lorrie, 6, 156

L
"La Fille aux Cheveux de Lin," 63
Lake Health, 7–8
LaRoche, Loretta, 14
Larson, Sharon, 4, 156
Lazarus, R., 159
LeDoux, J., 158
Lehrer, P. M., 159
Les Misérables, 123
lessons, 134
music, 105–6
*Let's Improvise: Becoming Creative,
Expressive and Spontaneous
through Drama* (Polsky), 159
Levitin, D. J., 159
Levkoff, S. E., 159
Lewinsohn, P. M., 159
Lewis, Z. A., 159
life, 3
life spans, 11
*The Listening Book: Discovering Your
Own Music* (Mathieu), 159
listening habits, 38
lithotripsy, 129
The Little Engine That Could
(Piper), 32
log sheets
Music Listening Log, 37–40, 48,
148, 166–67
Pain Assessment Log, 33–35, 48,
133–35
Stress Assessment Log, 27–32, 48,
162–63